TRANSFORM
YOUR LIFE

DEDICATION

This book is dedicated to my mum, Joan Winifred Shepherd, who taught me to never give up and to go after what you want. To change and adapt, to focus and, most importantly, to follow your intuition.
I'm sorry I let you down when you needed me.

TRANSFORM
YOUR LIFE

AFTER INJURY, MENTAL ILLNESS, OR IF YOU JUST DON'T LIKE THE LIFE YOU LIVE

ADAM BALDOCK

TRANSFORM YOUR LIFE
Adam Baldock

* * *

© Adam Baldock 2022

Set in Palatino Linotype

All rights reserved.
No part of this publication may be reproduced, stored in a retrieval system or transmitted in any form by any means without the prior permission of the copyright owner.
Enquiries should be made to the publisher.

www.firedupgroup.com.au

CONTENTS

INTRODUCTION 1

Chapter 1 - YOUR LIFE 5

Chapter 2 - OWNERSHIP 19

Chapter 3 - INTUITION 33

Chapter 4 - CHANGE 53

Chapter 5 - FOCUS 73

Chapter 6 - SELF-RELIANCE 93

Chapter 7 - TRANSFORM 111

REFERENCES 125

INTRODUCTION

Take action toward your goals and you will achieve them.

– Joan Winifred Shepherd

My mum was a strong woman. The oldest of nine and a beauty contest winner, I am told. Whilst I know little about her early years, I do know that she and my father met when Mum was in her teens and Poppa (Mum's father) would not let them marry until Mum turned twenty-one.

I have three older siblings. The closest is thirteen years older than me. By the time I was old enough to know I had siblings, they had all left home and I was practically raised as an only child.

By all accounts, Mum and Dad were happy for most of their marriage but when Dad, a serial entrepreneur, lost all the family money for the third time (I still remember the repo men taking the furniture out of the house), Mum decided she'd had enough. She left Dad and took me with her.

The stress of it all got to Mum and she had to spend a little time in hospital. Close to a year, I think (you don't track time when you are only seven). Whilst she recovered, I lived with my aunty in a small dam-building town of Twizel in the central South Island of New Zealand. Twizel was a tough town and I got my arse kicked at school nearly every day. It wasn't the happiest of times, but I can't say I was miserable. After all, I had the regular torment inflicted by my older cousins (all in fun) to take my mind off it.

Whilst most psychologists would espouse this as a traumatic period in my life causing me great stress and mental anguish,

I don't remember it that way. I simply lived with my aunty and when Mum was better, we moved houses and then we moved cities. I lived with Mum full time, and saw Dad every four weeks. He worked as a traveling confectionary salesperson with a territory that had him come through town on a four-week rotation, and I spent most of the school holidays traveling with him. I got to try new confections before any other kid. What more would you want? I wasn't unhappy. In fact, I see my upbringing as positive in most instances. So, I surmise that Mum, Dad, and my Aunty Kate did a good job at working together and sparing me from any unpleasantness.

In my opinion, Mum did a great job raising me and, as I said in the dedication at the start of this book, taught me right from wrong, tenacity, to chase my goals, adapt to change, and to follow my dreams. I inherited a lot of good things from my mum... some not so good things too.

Mum would always sweat the small stuff, getting quite emotional about caring for your clothes, eating your veg etcetera. She was a little intense that way, but give her a full-blown crisis and she was cool, calm and collected. The all-knowing guru on what to do. I got both these traits, but I wish I hadn't inherited the former. She supported me through my school years, even though it would appear I was quite dumb. When she passed away, we found all my school reports. They in no way reflect a future in academia.

She helped me get my first job. Working to the small hours creating a pitch to the employer and making me remember it. They loved it and I got the job. She was always there when I needed her. It is a shame I did not reciprocate.

You see, when Mum was sixty-five (I was about twenty-two) she had a massive stroke. Her worst nightmare. Unfortunately, the doctors had trouble stabilising her and she spent months in hospital with a piece of her skull removed to compensate for the swelling before spending more time in rehabilitation as both an inpatient and then as an outpatient. Her nine siblings all put in for a private intensive rehabilitation program and Mum returned to a point where she could stand again (not walk) and was returning to some level of independence.

This, in hindsight, is where I should have stepped in. Had I done so and managed her rehabilitation, ensured she completed her daily exercises and limit her drinking and smoking, she might have been around a bit longer. More importantly, she might have lived out her final eight years in happiness. Not the hell in which her stroke condemned her.

In this book you are going to read about owning your situation, the impact of your environment, and being able to make change. You are going to read about what it takes to transform your life in any circumstance. How, whilst you need to be self-resilient, you also need to rely on your networks and the people who love you, to help. My self-interest at the time meant Mum didn't get the support she probably so desperately sought from me when she needed it.

This combined with her unsupportive husband (Mum remarried), refusing to help her with her exercises and providing an environment of alcoholism and indolence, Mum deteriorated and in a brief period required admittance to 24-hour care in an aged care facility. Trapped in her body with only her rosary beads and our sporadic (family) visits to keep her company, she eventually willed herself to death some eight years after her original brain haemorrhage. Eight years in prison. A prison I may have been able to free her from with love and support. The same love and support she gave me and the five things I discuss in this book, that I now know could have saved her from the misery of those final years.

Don't get me wrong, I am not saying I am completely at fault. Mum, too, had a responsibility to help herself. As she used to say: *'take action toward your goals and achieve them'.* By the way, I am not sure it is her quote, but she used to say it often enough, so as far as I am concerned, she owns it. Mum had to cross the Five Bridges espoused in this book. Unfortunately, one or more of those bridges was a bridge too far.

My point is, as an occupational therapist and knowing what I know now, I should have pushed Mum to cross these bridges, as she pushed me on so many occasions. If I had, just maybe, her final years might have been better.

So, this book is dedicated to my mum, Joan Winifred Shepherd. A great woman who is responsible for you being able to make the transformation she could not. For you being able to understand what it takes to transform your life after injury, illness, or if you just don't like the life you live. She is a woman that would sit up all night to help you understand the opportunity these pages afford you. So don't let her down.

Chapter 1

YOUR LIFE

You can't wait until life isn't hard anymore until you decide to be happy.

– Jane Marczewski (aka Nightbirde)

~ 1 ~

Long before she took on the name *'Nightbirde'*, Jane Marczewski dreamed of becoming a singer as a little girl growing up in Zanesville, Ohio. Jane graduated from Lincoln Valley Acaemy in 1989 and later that year began attending Liberty University as an advertising and public relations student. It was during that time at Liberty that she was first encouraged to pursue music professionally.

At Liberty she was constantly challenged with the question: "If you could do anything for this world and you knew you would succeed, what would you do?" For Jane, the answer was always music. But she never felt it was a realistic path before attending Liberty. She explained, "Lynchburg and those beautiful mountains, it's where I found myself really and where I found my voice and it was such a launching pad for me that I'll be grateful for that forever. I don't know where I'd be had I not started my music career in Lynchburg."

Jane auditioned for Liberty's traveling music teams but never seemed to make the cut. Undeterred, Jane began writing her own music and in 2011 she recorded three original songs and played her first show at the Whiteheart Café.

In 2013 she released her debut EP – 'Ocean & Sky'. She began developing a following in the Lynchburg area and even made the cover of *Lynchburg Living Magazine* in 2014. Off stage, however, Jane was struggling with the pressure of her success. "Along with the successes," she claimed, "came the fear that I would be found out. Just the sense, that oh, my gosh, everybody thinks that I am so amazing, but I'm not really that amazing, so I need to keep everyone at a distance."

After a performance downtown one Friday night, Jane made the decision to step away from music for a couple of months and return home to Ohio. Two months turned into a year, and she met and fell in love with fellow musician Jeremy Claudio. Eight months later they married, then moved to Nashville soon after.

Jane decided to restart her music career and took on the new stage name 'Nightbirde'. Her stage name was inspired by a reoccurring dream of birds singing at her window. One morning the dream was so vivid that she got up to look out the window and there was, in fact, three birds singing in the dawn, even though there was no hint of dawn on the horizon.

In early 2017 as she became comfortable with the idea of performing again, she was diagnosed with breast cancer. In the following months Jane underwent three rounds of chemotherapy which included three additional surgeries resulting in a double mastectomy.

In July 2017 Jane received news that her cancer was in remission. As she was ready to start to perform again a follow up exam in November 2017 revealed new symptoms. Scans showed three tumours in her spine, three more in her lungs and numerous tumours in her liver and throughout her ribs. On New Year's Eve 2019, she was diagnosed with terminal cancer. Just days later her husband left their marriage and the couple divorced a few weeks later.

Jane was given three to six months to live, but survived

much longer with the help of a new treatment she received in California. She said, "after the doctors told me I was dying and the man I married told me he didn't love me anymore, I chased a miracle in California, and I got it." By July 2020, Jane's cancer was again in remission.

Unfortunately, Jane's battle with the disease wasn't quite over. Later that year a follow up exam revealed the cancer had again returned. In a blog post she wrote, 'I have had cancer three times now and I am barely past 30. There are times in my life when I wonder what I must have done to deserve such a story.'

Throughout her battle with cancer Jane continued to produce music and has released three originals to streaming platforms including the song she is most well-known for 'It's OK'. She recently released a live version of the song and performed the single in her audition for America's Got Talent (AGT). Before her audition Jane told judges that she was performing an original song that she wrote about her battle with cancer and her determination to remain positive. Judge, Simon Cowell then asked how she was doing now, and she responded that the last time she checked she had some cancer in her lungs, spine, and liver. The following exchange took place between Judge, Howie Mandel and Jane:

Howie: "So, you're not OK."

Jane (calmly): "well, not in every way, no!"

Howie: "You have a beautiful glow and a beautiful smile, and no one would know."

Jane: *"It's important that people know I am so much more than the bad things that happen to me."*

Jane then gave a moving performance and was given the covered 'Golden Buzzer' sending her straight to the live shows. After the performance, Jane told, AGT host Terry Cruise, "I have a two percent chance of survival, but two percent is not zero percent. Two percent is something and I wish people knew how amazing it is."

(YouTube, 2021)

~ 2 ~

You are so much more than the bad things that happen to you! If you have chosen to pick up this book, then I can only assume that your life is not what you would like it to be, and you are looking for some help to transform your life. Maybe you have sustained an injury and for whatever reason you can't return to your previous style of living. Maybe you have experienced a period of ill mental health and you need a change to reset and restart your life in a more positive sense. Or maybe you just don't like where you currently are in life, and you just need a change. Whatever your reason for picking up this book, I want to congratulate you – you've come to the right place!

Every year, over 532,500 cases of injury result in admission to hospital in Australia. The rate of hospitalised injury is >2,148 per 100,000 population. The main causes of hospitalised injury are falls (42%), followed by injury due to inanimate mechanical forces (14%), and transport crashes (12%).

Most injuries, whether unintentional or intentional, are preventable (WHO 2014). Despite this, every year in Australia, thousands of people die and many more are admitted to hospital or attend hospital emergency departments. While people with minor injuries typically recover completely, those who survive serious injuries often have lasting health problems (Gabbe et al., 2017).

Injuries can happen to anyone, but some population groups are more at risk than others, such as people who live in more remote areas or have a lower socioeconomic position, Aboriginal and Torres Strait Islander peoples.

In 2015, injuries accounted for 8.5% of the burden of disease in Australia (AIHW 2019b) and 7.0% of the long-term health conditions of the more than 4.3 million Australians living with a disability (ABS 2016). Injury is one of the top five contributing categories to the national burden of disease, along with cancer, cardiovascular diseases, musculoskeletal conditions, and mental and substance use disorders (AIHW 2019b).

In 2015–16, it was estimated that injury cost the Australian health system $8.9 billion dollars, which amounts to 7.6% of total health expenditure (AIHW 2019a). In 2017–18, the average length of stay in hospital for injury cases was 3.8 days—a total of almost 1.8 million days in hospital was recorded (AIHW 2020a) and we haven't even touched on mental health.

Mental health is a key component of overall health and wellbeing (WHO, 2013). The National Survey of Mental Health and Wellbeing conducted in 2007 found that an estimated 1 in 5 (20%) Australians aged 16–85 experienced a mental disorder in the previous 12 months (ABS, 2008). A mental illness can be defined as: *'a clinically diagnosable disorder that significantly interferes with a person's cognitive, emotional, or social abilities'* (COAG Health Council, 2017). The term itself covers a range of illnesses including anxiety disorders, affective disorders, psychotic disorders, and substance use disorders.

However, a person does not need to meet the criteria for a mental illness or mental disorder to be negatively affected by their mental health (COAG Health Council, 2017; Slade et al. 2009). Mental health effects and is affected by multiple socioeconomic factors including a person's access to services, living conditions and employment status, and affects not only the individual but also their families and carers (Slade et al. 2009; WHO, 2013).

The National Survey of Mental Health and Wellbeing 2007 estimated that:
- Nearly 1 in 2 (46%) Australians aged 16–85 had experienced a mental disorder during their lifetime
- 1 in 5 (20%) people who had experienced a mental disorder in their lifetime had symptoms in the 12 months prior to the

survey interview. Of those, anxiety disorders were the most prevalent type of disorder (14%), followed by affective disorders (6.2%) and substance use disorders (5.1%)
- A higher proportion of males than females (48% compared with 43%) had experienced a mental disorder in their lifetime; however, a higher proportion of females than males (22% compared with 18%) had experienced symptoms in the 12 months prior to the survey
- 16–24-year-olds (26%) were most likely to have experienced symptoms of a mental disorder in the previous 12 months and those aged 75–85, the least likely (5.9%)
- Over 4 in 10 (43%) people with a disability status of profound or severe core-activity limitation experienced symptoms of a mental disorder in the 12 months before the survey, compared with 17% of people with no disability or limitations (ABS 2008)

The Australian Child and Adolescent Survey of Mental Health and Wellbeing 2013–14 (Young Minds Matter) estimated that, in the 12 months before the survey:
- 560,000 children and adolescents aged 4–17 (14%) experienced a mental disorder
- Males had a higher prevalence of mental disorders (16%) than females (12%)
- Of the mental disorders experienced by participants, the following were most prevalent: attention deficit hyperactivity disorder (ADHD) (7.4%); anxiety disorders (6.9%); major depressive disorder (2.8%); and conduct disorder (2.1%). (Lawrence et al. 2015)

Sorry for all the stats, but they do paint the picture for the rest of the book. Last set of stats.

The National Health Survey 2017–18 estimated that:
- 1 in 5 (20%, or 4.8 million) Australians reported a mental

or behavioural condition during the collection period (July 2017 to June 2018)
- Females reported a higher proportion of mental or behavioural conditions (22%) than males (18%)
- Overall, 15–24-year-olds had the highest proportion of mental or behavioural conditions (26%) and 0–14-year-olds had the lowest (11%)
- Of those participants who had a severe disability, 58% had a mental or behavioural condition compared with 14% of those with no disability or long-term restrictive health condition (ABS 2018)

The deterioration of Australian mental health as depicted by these three surveys is prolific, and it continues to grow year on year. Even without events like COVID to exacerbate.

When I started my occupational therapy career in 1999, mental health conditions were all but a non-existing issue. It was all physical injury. And despite occupational therapy training purporting to be a holistic education, considering the entire needs of the patient, a patient's mental health after injury was seldom considered.

~ 3 ~

I was drawn to occupational therapy in my young teenage years after watching a movie (I can't even remember the name of it) where the protagonist experiences an accident and is paralysed. In the scene that set my destiny, the protagonist is lying in his hospital bed, a quadriplegic (unable to move from the neck down) and either the OT or the Physiotherapist comes in, introduces himself, picks up our hero's limp arm and drops it, allowing the hand to drop on to his, with the therapist proclaiming *'high-five – I am the man who is going to get you living again'*. Whilst it sounds a bit off to be doing that to a patient, it set my mind racing. Wouldn't it be cool if you could get someone walking again after an accident?

That is where it started and whilst I forgot about it for a few years, I came back to it in 1995 after realising my career path in hospitality would not take me where I wanted to go. I guess you could say this was one of my life transformations. Not my first, but certainly one of the more profound.

I graduated as an occupational therapist in New Zealand in 1999. I went straight into injury management with Aon Insurance, managing the rehabilitation of people post injury. About a year later I was chosen to be part of the team to set up Cambridge Workcover Insurance (now known as DXC) in Melbourne, Australia. Australia is where I have lived ever since.

I've worked for insurance companies' rehabilitation providers, safety organisations, I've found, grown and sold an paediatric occupational therapy and speech pathology clinic and started an injury management consultancy providing injury management advice to many of Australia's most well-known organisations. I also work with law firms to provide medico-legal assessment and contract my services for injury management (both physical and psychological) to insurance companies. I collaborate with an awesome team of health professionals to provide business coaching to those who have experienced physical or psychological injury and can no longer run their business. We help them to adjust their lives and/or their business to accommodate their physical or psychological needs.

I love my job. There is nothing like seeing a person who thought everything was over, transform their life into the dream they never knew they had.

I wouldn't change my career and while it hasn't always been rosy, right now as I write this book, I would not want to be doing anything else. How did I get here? Well, that is what you are about to learn from this book. This is not just my interpretation via my work but I, too, have had to cross each of the bridges discussed here to discover what I really wanted in life and how to get it. I must admit, it hasn't come easy. It has required a lot of work, and I don't have an injury or a mental health condition impacting my progress. But having transformed my life several times throughout my period on this planet, and having worked with thousands of people to help them transform their lives, I can tell you, it is hard!

According to numerous scientific studies, only 8% of people consider themselves successful, living the way they want and doing what they want to be doing. Just 8%. That's a miniscule number. That means 92% of people wish their lives were different. Why don't they just make a change? Truth be told, most of them probably don't know how. And that is why I have written this book.

This book considers my 21-plus years of injury management and occupational rehabilitation experience as well as my own experiences of transformation; the thousands of people I have worked with, the ones that have transformed their lives and the ones that found the bridge too hard to cross. Their fear got the better of them. Where in reality and, in all likelihood, if they had crossed that bridge, it would have transformed their life and made the change they sought.

~ 4 ~

Why bridges? To answer that we need to consider what a bridge is. While we know a bridge as many things: a structure traversing a river, road, or other obstacle; the elevated, enclosed platform on a ship; the part of a stringed instrument over which the strings are stretched, just to name a few. It is also something intended to reconcile or connect two seemingly incompatible things. When we cross a bridge, we are often crossing a caesium between two varying parts of the world, two different countries or two different pieces of land – the place we are to the place we want to be.

A bridge joins two places so that we can continue our journey. We can move forward. But to move forward we *need* to cross the bridge. If the bridge is broken or washed out, then we are stuck on this side of the caesium until we can find a way to fix the bridge and continue our journey to the other side.

This can be seen as a metaphor for life, and certainly a metaphor for this book. On life's journey we often have events that happen *to* us or *for* us, depending on which way you view life. We must journey through these events to reach a point where we can move forward. Sometimes these events are minor, and we simply brush them off and continue on. Other times, however, these events are large and can stall our journey whilst we deal with them before continuing our journey once again. There are also times when these events are catastrophic and require us to re-evaluate our journey altogether. No matter how small or large the event, we need to reach certain places—either physically or mentally, sometimes both—to be able to move forward. To reach those places we need to journey across a bridge that takes us from where we are to where we want to be.

This book is about the bridges people need to cross to transform their life, to move to their dream place. The place they want to be. The space between and the activities that need to be completed to connect those places are the *bridges*.

~ 5 ~

I have been an occupational therapist, rehabilitation consultant and business coach for over 21 years. I have worked with thousands of people who have experienced many kinds of life-events. Some of these events have been small, some large and others catastrophic; each handled differently by the people who experience them. All these events stalled the person, leaving them stuck on the side of the caesium they don't want to be. All of them required a bridge to enable them to continue their journey.

As you read these pages, you will meet a few of these people. Some are successful in their transformation, others are not and may well be still trapped on the side of the caesium they don't wish to be.

For the ones still trapped, it is likely they simply can't get out of their own way to cross the bridge. As an outsider, it is obvious as to why they have not yet been able to continue their journey and you will pull at your hair, as I have, in frustration. Luckily, I have been blessed with good, thick hair genes, so I can afford to pull a few out.

In part, this inability to cross the bridge is not their fault; their environment, upbringing, and the people they associate with have taught them over many years that someone else is to blame for their situation, and they may even conspire to make that person pay thus distracting them from moving forward. Eventually, they will need to move past this way of thinking to get on with life. This book will show them—and you—how.

Earlier I suggested that I have helped the people I have worked with to transform their lives into the dream life they never knew they wanted. I suggested they may have already had the knowledge and the vision of what they want in life, they just did not know how to get there. This book will teach you how to tap into your unknown life desires. The desires you think you never knew you had but did. That part of you that craves something different or the ability to just move forward with what you have.

Well, I am here to tell you that you already know what you want. You already know how to get it. You just need the inspiration and insight to appreciate it. This book will help you recognise your pathway to your transformed life. The life that is already within you. You just need to set it free.

This book is not focussed on change; however, change is a big part of this book. Is there something in your life that you don't like? Something that has happened to put you in a position of discontent? Something that is stopping you from living your best life ever? Whether it is injury, mental health or just plain life-dissatisfaction, you will need to make a change. A change for the better. One to accommodate your physical capability or your mental state. A change to assimilate into your life your ongoing health and/or general needs. This book will help you do that.

Upon hearing this you may start to doubt your ability to tap into your life's desires and make that change. You may think about all the times you have started something only to give up. Another New Year's resolution that never eventuated. You may be in pain, depressed, you are most definitely anxious about the prospect of having to actually do something. To focus and see something through. To not give up when it gets tough. I am here to tell you, you can do it. And I am going to show you how to focus on the end goal and step into your new, transformed life.

The people in this book, the ones that have been successful in transforming their lives, have all been where you are right now or where you may have been. Remember, you may already be part way through your transformational journey. If these people can do it, so can you. You are not alone.

Finally, I am going to show you how you can tap into the resources around you – the friends, colleagues and family members who are just waiting to help you live the transformed life you are looking for. These people want the best for you and will walk over broken glass to help you get there. You just don't know it yet, and you owe it to yourself and to them to give it your best.

There is also a world of people you don't know that are equally willing to walk across fire (Tony Robbins style) to help you live transformed. Imagine that! A group of complete strangers just waiting to help you. You just need to show them you are ready.

TRANSFORM YOUR LIFE

This book is the start of your journey… or at least the start of your realisation that you need to take those first steps on a voyage to a new life. You will cross five bridges that, from my 21 years in helping people transform their lives after injury or ill mental health, are the Five Bridges all the people who have successfully transformed their lives, have crossed. If you can cross these bridges with me, then I guarantee you will Transform Your Life.

It's your life – it is time to do something with it.

Chapter 2

OWNERSHIP

We are solely responsible for our choices, and we have to accept the consequences of every deed, word, and thought throughout our lifetime.

– Elizabeth Kuber-Ross

Spoiler Alert – The first section of this chapter discusses a scene from the Netflix Series *Ozark*. If you intend to watch it and don't want me to spoil some of the plot I suggest you start at section two in this chapter.

~ 1 ~

In the Netflix series *Ozark*, Marty Byrd is a financial advisor who launders money for a Mexican cartel. After his business partner is caught skimming and subsequently killed, the always calm and quick-thinking Marty uses a brochure in his pocket to convince the cartel to spare him and his family's lives and set up the money laundering in the Ozarks (a lake district in Minnesota, United States).

Marty moves the family to the Ozarks and successfully starts to launder money for the cartel. As you might expect, Marty is faced with an endless set of challenges which include a poppy-growing and heroin-manufacturing hillbilly who is less than happy with Marty encroaching on his turf, and a family of criminal rednecks seeking to kill Marty and steal the cartel's money.

During the story, Marty accidentally hinders the hillbilly's distribution through a local church and informs a previously unaware preacher of the illegal activities occurring amongst his congregation. The preacher then refuses to hold service but is encouraged by the hillbillies to re-ignite his preaching. The preacher, unaware of the likely outcome, continues to refuse. Marty attempts to assist with a monetary incentive to the hillbillies and for a period stave off the preacher's execution.

Still, the preacher refuses and the hillbillies decide they 'have been clear and they have been patient'. One day, the Preacher comes home to find his pregnant wife gone and a newborn baby wrapped in a blanket on the kitchen table. Despite these events, the preacher still refuses to return to services and again Marty pays off the hillbillies in an effort for them to not kill the man, yet the preacher exacerbates the situation by refusing to accept help from any source and ends up living on the street with his newborn. Social welfare then takes the child. Desperate, the preacher commits his own crimes and ends up being killed.

Marty is later asked about why he seems completely emotionless about the preacher, although it should be noted that the Preacher's death did have a major impact on Marty as he personally killed the man. All the other people Marty has witnessed killed were done so at the hands of the cartel, the hillbillies and the redneck crime family. Marty's answer to the aforementioned question: *'we all make choices, and those choices have consequences. All those people made a choice.'*

Marty's point is solid. Everything we do, we choose to do. Everything that happens to us in life, even when it does not feel like it, we somehow made choices that brought us to that event – good or bad.

However, what I now increasingly see is the lack of accountability, the lack of ownership for those choices. In my view it feels as though everybody is looking for someone to blame for their selections particularly where those choices have not had the expected outcome.

~ 2 ~

David was a graphic designer who experienced the onset of a mental health episode when the landlord of his business premises attempted to evict him. David perceived that he was being bullied and harassed. He reported experiencing anxiety and depression and drew on his income protection policy. At the time, he was living with his family in Perth and decided to move back to Melbourne to be closer to his ageing parents. David's insurance company engaged me to help him find a pathway to return to work.

I first met David in a building (formerly a dry-cleaning business, owned by his parents) that he was renovating with the hope of opening an art gallery and artist workspace. The building was quite large, and he had visions of adding a café and marketplace.

At the time of our initial meeting David had not worked for two years. He told me that he did not believe he could return to work in graphic design because he had not, and was not interested in upskilling, to be able to use computer-based software. He was also reluctant to do web-based work which was a large portion of the work in this sector, particularly in this online environment we live in. David wanted 6-12 months to try and build the art gallery.

David was under the care of a psychologist but as our work together continued and, unbeknown to me, he let the psychologist go and was not receiving any treatment. Progress on the business was slow and he always seemed to have an excuse for not completing key tasks to move the business forward. The biggest barrier to his success was his lack of funds. He had no money to market the business, complete a proper and attractive fit-out of the premise or attract artists and/or subleases for the intended café space. Even if someone had shown interest in subleasing and setting up a café, David had no money to bring the part of the building proposed for the café back to base in preparation for the café. It was clear to everyone, except David, that he could not move forward.

I proposed that we return him to work in some format and that his earnings from his employment could aid the development of his dream. David reluctantly agreed. I engaged a Job Search specialist to help find a role and whilst we did find David some employment there was always a reason he could not take the employment on.

In the meantime, I discovered he had not had any treatment – psychological or other – for almost a year and had stopped all medication. Working together with his former rehabilitation team I re-introduced David to treatment, and he did stabilise for a period. However, for some reason, one that I could never figure out, he would not take any of the employment opportunities and always had a personal crisis—trying to sell his house in Perth, parents wanting to sell the proposed art gallery building etc.,—that stopped him from moving forward.

About 18 months into my work with David, I discovered he still retained the lease of his business premise in Perth and that throughout this time, things had laid dormant. So, David had not done anything about it. Now the landlord was looking to evict David and retain a new tenant. When I asked David why he had not exited the lease when he had the opportunity and/or not done anything about it, let alone mention it to me, his answer floored me. David said, "Because I want him to pay for what he has done to me." David had not accepted what had happened to him and not moved on. This was the long-lost reason as to why I had been struggling to place David in work or upgrade his rehabilitation.

It was this moment that I realised I could not help David at this time. He required counselling and psychological input to *process* his experience, work through it and reach a point where he could look forward, not back. I organised for his referral to the appropriate health specialists and withdrew from the file.

TRANSFORM YOUR LIFE

~ 3 ~

You can see from the above anecdote that the choices David made throughout his therapy with me, exacerbated his condition. Equally, David wanted someone else to take the blame for his choices, and whilst perseverating on who he felt was responsible, stopped himself from moving forward.

This example helps us realise that until you can accept your circumstance, and that in some way you made choices that resulted in your current reality, it is difficult to see a future.

So, we reach the first bridge that needs to be crossed in the process of transforming your life: Ownership.

Why is it so hard for some of us to accept events? Particularly when those events feel unjust? Some people can! They do and move on just fine. I can certainly give you examples of people I have worked with both in rehabilitation and/or business coaching that make extraordinary recoveries or changes to their lives after experiencing the most horrific of circumstance. Alan Newey is a prime example and someone you will read about later in this book. Their ability to own their circumstance is the answer. That said, it is not easy for everyone. I'd be out of a job if it were!

There are several reasons people fail to accept or own their circumstance. This book is not long enough to talk about them all. I can only talk about the ones that seem to affect my clients. The barriers to their dream life. Yes, I am talking about Regret, Guilt and Shame.

We all mess up sometimes. Whether it's lashing out at a friend, engaging in self-destructive behaviour or cutting corners at work. With those mistakes often come overwhelming feelings of guilt, shame, self-condemnation, and humiliation. Counsellors and life coaches have found that these emotions can lead to stress, depression, anxiety disorders and even heart disease, if ignored. But as you will see in future chapters, it is also a cause for mental health disorder and procrastination.

As an occupational therapist, rehabilitation consultant and business coach, I can help people like David process events. Usually, we talk the situation through. As the therapist, I implant or lead the client to their own solution. The outcome is always better when the client reaches their own solution. If they don't work it through, can't process it, or the event is so embedded, so entrenched that they just can't move forward, then I need to refer them to someone with expertise in helping someone process the deep stuff. Often, we work with these other disciplines, continuing our rehabilitation program in a multi-disciplinary approach. The results are often better than one-to-one therapy.

If you are reading this book because you want to transform your life, you don't like where you are at in life or have experienced an event that has forced your hand and you now need to transform to live, then telling you that you need to just process the event to move forward is not going to make it happen. You need to understand how you got here, how (if you have) reached rock bottom, and how you can work it through. So, let's look at how therapy works and how it helps to move you forward.

To explore this area, we will look at the work of Dr Noam Shpancer (Ph.D.), a professor of psychology at Otterbein College and a practising clinical psychologist in Columbus, Ohio, who has written about how events are processed and how therapy works. He proposes that humans process events in five ways:

1. Working to place the event inside a coherent life narrative. In other words, placing the event within our life story.
2. Bringing past events or habits into present consciousness and analysing them using our current tools and knowledge, resulting in fresh insight.
3. Through the prism of cognitive developmental theory. Creating 'Schemas' as proposed in the pioneering work of cognitive theorist, Jean Piaget.
4. By engaging it, thinking, and talking about it. In doing so, we are practising exposure with regard to the emotions attached

to the issue and can learn to manage those emotions; and
5. Bringing the issue into the light of another's benevolent attention.

According to Shpancer, by processing in these contexts, events can be viewed as a way to familiarise a person with unfamiliar territory. When we process an issue, we learn the terrain, thereby becoming less afraid of it and more able to navigate within it.

Let us go a little deeper and explore each one of these processing techniques (often used in collaboration with each other) individually.

Working to place the event inside a coherent life narrative.
As humans we tend to experience our life as a story. In most instances we are the protagonist, heroically moving forward. When we meet people we become the narrator, telling others about our experience to date and what that has meant to us. This is how we help people understand who we are, and when we hear the narrative of others' lives, this is how we understand them.

When an event occurs that is outside how we see ourselves and/or our story or we become overwhelmed by the event (you can't stop thinking about it and it affects your ability to function) we need to process the event. Therapy, in this instance, works by integrating the event into our story or removing it from the story all together. Not easily achievable on its own. So, it needs to be combined with one or more of the other processing tools.

Bringing past events or habits into present consciousness and analysing them using our current tools and knowledge, resulting in fresh insight.
Avoidance is the key aspect here. Traumatic events often cause a person to avoid emotions, places and memories associated with that event. When people frequent these places, they tend to up-

date the file in their brain to incorporate their associated new thoughts, feelings and memories.

When avoiding, people fail to re-evaluate, explore or change their thoughts, feelings and memories with any new information or knowledge associated with the traumatic event or place. This means the event stays, as experienced (frozen in time) and thus the person has difficulty moving forward. The person's repertoire of reacting to similar situations and events is limited to their original reaction, which may be no longer appropriate.

Take for example a young child who falls in the swimming pool and near drowns. They may avoid all forms of water and are therefore unable to realise that water can be fun, relaxing and therapeutic. Therapy in this case requires the person to test the reality of the information they have on the event and adopt the new information to move forward.

In this technique the therapist would look to re-examine the emotions and memories associated with the event and change the way the event is described to bring it from the past to the present context.

This is where a person needs to change their schemas.

Through the prism of cognitive developmental theory.
The pioneering cognitive theorist, Jean Piaget proposed that as children we learn by interacting with the world, exploring our environment, and experimenting with our behaviour to understand how things work. By undertaking these explorations and experimenting we gain a library of knowledge, which Piaget calls '*schemas*', which are effectively organised ways of how to interact with the world in various situations.

An example being attendance at a café. If you are an integrated Melburnian (or live in any Australian city for that matter) you understand what to do and what will happen when you attend a café for a coffee. You know how to order, how the wait staff will attend to you and the things you must do to be socially accepted in this environment. You have a 'café schema'. When you attend a café that does not operate in the expected way, e.g., requires you to order at the counter as opposed to table service etc., you update your 'café schema' accordingly for the next time you attend that café.

Now Piaget proposed that schemas are formulated in two ways: Assimilation and Accommodation.

Assimilation is where we use an existing schema to understand new information. Accommodation on the other hand is where the new information does not fit with any of our existing schemas, and we must adjust to accept this new information.

Shpancer gives a great example of accommodation with a high level of relevance in our multi-cultural, gender-diverse world for today. If your wife gives birth to a new baby boy, assimilating him into your 'male family member' schema will be easy. Yet if your adult daughter decides to transition to become a man, then you may need to accommodate your old 'male family member' schema to include transgender persons.

So, the therapist using this technique seeks to help the patient to assimilate or accommodate new information to move past the traumatic event and move through the world with greater ease.

But to truly process the event you still need to think and talk about it.

By engaging it, thinking, and talking about it.

In doing this a client is, in essence, exposed repeatedly to the event and over time somewhat desensitised as they learn to deal with it psychologically and learn new behaviours when exposed to such stimuli. By confronting the memories and emotions, the client gains an increased sense of achievement and proficiency and with it a reduction in symptoms.

With even more exposure the client learns to associate differently to the situation or stimulus. Taking the swimming example from earlier, by slowly increasing exposure to the water the person learns that they can float and not drown in water.

A real-life example of this situation is Tim Ferris, the author of *'The Four-Hour Work Week'* who was afraid of water and only learned to swim in his late-30's. He found it one of the hardest things he had ever attempted. This coming from a man that created a TV series where he had to learn how to cage fight in seven days before being matched against a professional fighter.

Therapy in this context means the client is increasingly made more familiar with unfamiliar thoughts, feelings, and emotions. As they become more familiar, they are better prepared to manage.

Talking about it with your therapist and making it part of your core group of friends are two different things and therefore the final step of therapy is…

Bringing the issue into the light of another's benevolent attention.
As social beings we tend to measure ourselves by others and, in particular, the response of others. By speaking to friends and family about the issue, you bring the problem into your network and the support of that network. This is communicating the issue in a safe environment where connection and understanding is gained. The importance of networks is discussed in more depth later in this book. Watch this space.

As the saying goes: *'A problem shared is a problem halved'*. If you share it enough the problem will be diminished to nothing or at the very least to a manageable part. One being managed by more than just you.

For best results, the problem needs to be shared with someone who has the capability of understanding the experience. By sharing our weakness, we gather strength.

Shpancer summarises it best:

'A secret loses much of its power to paralyse and poison us internally when shared with others who are capable of resonating with our experience, accepting and understanding it. In the act of discussing difficult matters, we become less alone, less opaque to ourselves, and thus less fragile. We manifest and build our strength when we express and own our weakness.'

~ 4 ~

We manifest and build our strength when we express and own our weakness. This is exactly what I see in my daily work. People beginning to reinvent themselves by owning their weakness. These people then manage to find something to compensate for that weakness, turning it into a strength. This is where working with rehabilitation consultants and business coaches like me, helps. Refuse to admit your weakness and you have moved into a mindset of victimisation. Exhibit A: David. In a victimisation mindset you cannot move forward as demonstrated earlier in this chapter.

It is an ego-swallowing challenge that is difficult for anyone, let alone someone who has experienced a life event that requires a major change. But if you are not going to take responsibility for your change, who is? It is not what you preach it is what you tolerate. If other people see that you tolerate your circumstance, then they will assume your circumstances are tolerable and not render any assistance when asked. It is a case of the boy who cried wolf. Talk about what you don't like about your life for too long without actioning change, people will stop listening.

There is, of course, one counter argument to this point. You need to be ready in mind and body to make that next step. We have seen from section three of this chapter that a big part of processing a life event is talking about it. Until a person has completed processing, they cannot move forward. So, the discussion may well be part of their reaching a point of ownership. Sooner or later, you must decide to make the change. This may need to occur before the processing is complete. Collin Powell, the former Secretary of Defence for the United States once said, "sometimes you need to take action with only forty percent of the information."

Now I am not suggesting that after partially working through an event you should make change. That is a great way to have a setback in your health. But preparing to make the change whilst processing the event can be therapeutic. Additionally, it helps you get to your goal sooner and make the change you so desperately seek. So, in essence, the sooner you can get to work on processing and ultimately owning your circumstance the sooner you can transform your life.

There is something empowering about ownership and making the decision to change your unwanted circumstance. By making these decisions you give yourself the opportunity to take credit for creating your own life. When you create your own life, you have the chance to increase your happiness and overall love for life. This happiness and love then spread amongst the universe, and you will find that new and often unexpected opportunities come to you. As the saying goes: *'where your focus goes, the energy grows'*. Your positive energy is contagious, and your life becomes filled with positive people.

You need to remember throughout the process that whilst you may feel like all your decisions up to this point have been poor, by experiencing the disappointment that arises from making a decision with an outcome that is different from that expected, and by processing that decision you give yourself the opportunity to propel into a new level of emotional evolution. By moving to this new plain, you gain the opportunity to master the art of self-forgiveness.

Self-forgiveness is a big part of ownership. Twice yearly I am honoured to be part of the support team on the 'Man's Inner Journey' retreat. This event is run by the Melbourne Men's Group, a voluntary group of amazing guys that meet monthly to support each other in a non-judgemental environment and help each other to work through tough times (see 4 and 5 of the processing above).

The twice-yearly retreat that is 'Man's Inner Journey' takes 25 men through progressive processes designed to help each forgive themselves for the mistakes they feel they have made and learn about why they are the person they are. It truly is a life-changing experience for the participants. I know, I have done it twice. You must do the course twice to be able to serve on the support team. As a support team member, it is pure magic to watch the transformation of these men from when they arrive on the Friday to when they depart on the Sunday night. They leave forgiven and empowered to make positive change in their lives. These men own their lives when they finish the retreat.

It should be noted here that there is a similar course for the ladies called 'The Goddess Within'. You can find both at www.themelbournemensgroup.com.au.

Returning to the matter at hand, there are several other reasons why owning your decisions is good for you and helps you to move forward positively. First, when you are moving forward, you get to bask in the glory of a decision 'gone right'. For every failed decision, you will make a successful decision and if you really want to add a cliché… there are no mistakes, just experiences and these experiences allow you to recognise that you are not your decisions.

You are more than the bad things that happen to you.
– Nightbirde

Depending on your thought process, you will be able to see that every decision holds value and has made you the person you are. The person that all your family and friends love.

Most importantly, ownership means you can now move forward to bridge number two, ready to refine what you do want in your life.

Chapter 3

INTUITION

Have the courage to follow your heart and intuition. They somehow already know what you truly want to become. Everything else is secondary.

– Steve Jobs

~ 1 ~

On 11 June 2010 at 8.30am the Australian Special Forces, including Corporal Roberts-Smith, climbed aboard a "four, two package" – four Blackhawk helicopters to carry the men and two Apache gunships to provide support.

Assigned a high-priority mission in northern Kandahar, they were to capture or kill a high-ranking Taliban leader. The unit knew the target was important. What they didn't know was that he had come to meet with 10 other senior commanders who were protected by over 100 highly-experienced, battle-competent militia.

Upon reaching the target's location, the helicopters immediately took on heavy fire. Extreme evasive manoeuvring by the legendary US 101st Airborne pilots meant the Rocket Propelled Grenades (RPGs) being fired at the helicopters, missed. The fire storm was so intense that in an interview after the event, these highly-experienced pilots conceded that the incoming rockets and bullets were like nothing they'd ever experienced.

With the choppers on the ground, the ASF soldiers leapt from the helicopters. Already two of the soldiers had been wounded. Battling 4-to-1 odds of success, they were out-positioned and outgunned.

Although only 70 metres from the enemy, they were in somewhat open ground and being fired upon from a walled compound above. The fire raining down was so heavy the team could not physically stand up without being shot. Their only choice, to crawl forward.

Being shot at from three different machine gun nests, the unit managed to crawl forward to within 30 metres of the Taliban before they were cut off and could go no further. Knowing something had to be done, Corporal Roberts-Smith noticed a small outbuilding to the team's right that could possibly offer some cover.

Signalling his colleagues on the left and right of his intension to clear the building, they rose and put in covering fire whilst Corporal Roberts-Smith made a mad dash with bullets flying all around him to reach the building.

Once at the building, nothing more than a small run-down shed, not much bigger than an outhouse, Corporal Roberts-Smith started to clear the structure when the nasty end of an RPG launcher slowly protruded from the window right next to him. At that range, he was easily able to identify him as an armed insurgent, engage him at point blank and kill him immediately.

Roberts-Smith then held up a grenade. His fellow soldiers recognising what he wanted began a count to three. On three they would provide cover fire whilst Smith threw the grenade into the building. It all might sound quite easy but for this manoeuvre to work, Roberts-Smith's mates had to stand up in the immediate line of fire of three machine guns and literally risk life and/or limb.

TRANSFORM YOUR LIFE

Without hesitation his colleagues did exactly that, dropping a clip into the enemy position and allowing Roberts-Smith the time to get the grenade away. Unfortunately, to little or no affect.

Still pinned down by machine guns, the unit remained in deadly danger from enemy fire. Knowing they could not just sit there, Corporal Roberts-Smith's training kicked in and he made the decision that he wasn't going to do nothing. From his position by the outbuilding, he ran at the wall, directly into the path of two of the machine guns.

Reaching the wall, he engaged and killed the first machine gunner. He quickly continued a few more metres along the wall, reached and neutralised the second machine gun installation.

Corporal Roberts-Smith's actions in taking out two machine gun nests saved the lives of his unit and turned the tide of the battle to allow the unit to regain the initiative and keep things moving forward. With the enemy's focus on Roberts-Smith, the ASF Platoon Commander was able to throw a grenade and silence the third machine gun.

The battle continued for a further nine hours. At its end, there would be 22 Taliban dead and five captured including the intended target. Not one coalition soldier was lost.

For his courage and actions on that day, Corporal Roberts-Smith was awarded the Victoria Cross – the highest award for acts of bravery in wartime and awarded by the Queen. In an interview on the television news doco *Sunday Night*, not long after receiving the award he told Mike Willesee that having … "utter disregard for our own safety, is what we do… and that he was only doing what he was trained to do."

(*Sunday Night*)

~ 2 ~

There is a quotation often used by the military, and used by Special Forces and Navy Seals in particular:

'Under pressure, you don't rise to the occasion, you sink to the level of your training.'

This quote is by Archilochus, a Greek poet who, by all accounts, was never an actual soldier. However, ancient tradition required he fight for the Thracians. Apparently, he died when the Thracians were fighting against soldiers from the island of Naxos. Records show that it was during the early days of this campaign when he made the statement in question.

Natalie Frank, content writer for 'Quora', an online blog, researched the origins of the quote and suggests that these words imply that the ability to succeed is not based on some type of Godly superpower someone is born with, such that they can simply expect to succeed knowing it will happen due to their exceptional abilities. Rather, success is based on the human ability to train to the point that when faced with a critical situation where someone has practised responses so many times, it has become an immediate reaction occurring without thought. It becomes instinct rather than cognisant thinking.

This concept also applies to martial art. Where those practitioners who journey the distance and find inner peace have practised the moves so often that when faced with a mortal enemy, it is unconscious action and muscle memory that reacts to the perceived threat, to respond and neutralise the menace.

This type of thinking is exampled nicely by an experience of Larry Bird, the basketball legend of the LA Lakers and Boston Celtics. According to the story, Bird was recruited to endorse a product. Paid millions to do so, as they usually are. During shooting of the advertisement, Bird was required to miss the shot. Legend has it, that 60 takes were required before Bird could miss. Bird had practised so much, his mind and muscles so finely tuned to success that he could not miss. Unbelievable!

TRANSFORM YOUR LIFE

~ 3 ~

Gavin de Becker is quite possibly the world's leading authority on violence prediction and pre-incident indicators. He is the designer of the MOSAIC Threat Assessment System (MOSAIC), which is used to screen threats to high-ranking officials and government representatives. He has twice been appointed to the Advisory Board to the President of the United States. He has made appearances and shared his views on violence prevention on *60 Minutes*, *Oprah*, *Larry King* and *20/20*, just to name a few.

De Becker also works with victims of violence, extortion or threats to help them process and understand the events and/or identify perpetrators. De Becker opines that like Corporal Roberts-Smith, Archilochus, Kungfu masters and Larry Bird, your intuition will tell you what to do in times of trouble.

In his 2008 book *The Gift of Fear*, de Becker opens with the story of Sally, a woman who lived in a four-storey apartment building and who came home one night to find the apartment building's security door ajar. Apparently, this was not unusual because other residents had left the door ajar accidently. That in itself did not alarm her, and she ignored any concern her biological systems alighted. According to de Becker, Sally entered and locked the door behind her and, carrying her groceries, began the stair climb to her level-four apartment.

Halfway to the top, Sally dropped some groceries and a tin of cat food rolled back down the stairs. To Sally's surprise a voice called out, "got it" and a young man came up the stairs with the escaped item. According to de Becker, Sally told him that upon hearing the voice, she did not like it, but again chose to ignore any biological alerts. After a brief exchange and against Sally's better judgement, she did not want the stranger's help but social etiquette prevented her from being rude. Sally handed one of the grocery bags to this stranger. The stranger was then allowed to help carry the groceries up to her apartment. I think we can all see where this is going.

De Becker then writes that once at the apartment, the stranger agreed to put the groceries on the counter and leave. This, of course, did not occur and Sally endured a long period of violation. When the stranger was finished, he rose from the bed, closed the window, and told her to stay quiet and he would leave. According to the story, Sally knew that he wasn't going to leave and when he left the bedroom, she ghosted him down the hall. When he turned right into the kitchen, she turned left out of the apartment and to the safety of neighbours.

She later learned that her attacker had murdered his previous victim and that Sally's actions in ghosting her attacker down the hall had saved her life. Sally later recalled that she just knew he was going to kill her and she just knew what she had to do. De Becker writes that his client told him that it was like an out-of-body experience where her intuition spoke to her, telling her that if she kept quiet and trusted it, it (her intuition) would get her out of this situation.

~ 4 ~

There are very few people who have not heard of what we know as the fight or flight response. To recap, the fight or flight response (also called 'hyperarousal' or the 'acute stress response') is a physiological reaction that occurs in response to a perceived harmful event, attack, or threat to survival. It was first described by Walter Bradford Cannon, whose theory states that animals react to threats with a general discharge of the sympathetic nervous system, preparing the animal for fighting or fleeing. More specifically, the adrenal medulla produces a hormonal cascade that results in the secretion of catecholamine(s), especially norepinephrine and epinephrine. The hormones estrogen, testosterone, and cortisol, as well as the neurotransmitters dopamine and serotonin, also affect how organisms react to stress.

The reaction begins in the amygdala, which triggers a neural response in the hypothalamus. The initial reaction is followed by activation of the pituitary gland and secretion of the hormone ACTH. The adrenal gland is activated almost simultaneously via the sympathetic nervous system, and releases the hormone epinephrine. The release of chemical messengers results in the production of the hormone cortisol, which increases blood pressure, blood sugar, and suppresses the immune system. The initial response and subsequent reactions are triggered in an effort to create a boost of energy. This boost is activated by epinephrine binding to liver cells and the subsequent production of glucose. Additionally, the circulation of cortisol functions to turn fatty acids into available energy, which prepares muscles throughout the body for response. Catecholamine hormones, such as adrenaline (epinephrine) or noradrenaline (norepinephrine), facilitate immediate physical reactions associated with a preparation for muscular action – run or fight.

These actions include:
- Acceleration of heart and lung function
- Paling or flushing, or alternating between both
- Inhibition of stomach and upper-intestinal action to the point where digestion slows or stops
- General effect on the sphincters of the body – your arse tightens
- Constriction of blood vessels in many parts of the body
- Liberation of metabolic energy sources (particularly fat and glycogen) for muscular action
- Dilation of blood vessels for muscles
- Inhibition of the lacrimal gland (responsible for tear production) and salivation
- Dilation of pupil (mydriasis) for improved acuity
- Relaxation of bladder
- Inhibition of erection
- Auditory exclusion (loss of hearing)

- Tunnel vision (loss of peripheral vision)
- Disinhibition of spinal reflexes
- Shaking

The physiological changes that occur during the fight or flight response are activated in order to give the body increased strength and speed in anticipation of fighting or running. Some of the specific physiological changes and their functions include:

- Increased blood flow to the muscles activated by diverting blood flow from other parts of the body
- Increased blood pressure, heart rate, blood sugars, and fats in order to supply the body with extra energy
- The blood clotting function of the body speeds up in order to prevent excessive blood loss in the event of an injury sustained during the response
- Increased muscle tension in order to provide the body with extra speed and strength

Most people have at some stage in their life experienced this biological response to a perceived threat; real or not. It is the body's way of protecting itself. Some people in this situation will have frozen, some run, some fought, and some reacted with little conscious input to successfully get out of the situation without resorting to one of the first three. As so depicted by the recounted actions of Sally in the opening pages of de Becker's, *The Gift of Fear*.

All of these examples, Corporal Roberts-Smith's heroic actions in Kandahar, Natalie Franks research into non-conscious action inspired by the saying *'Under pressure, you don't rise to the occasion, you sink to the level of your training'*, the contemplation of masters of martial arts, Bird's unbelievable prowess on the basketball court and de Becker with victims of crime, all show a common theme of human nature. That is, our bodies and minds already know how to get out of trouble. We just need to listen more often.

But this is not as easy as you think. The human race has set in place a series of rules of behaviour. Rules that depict an acceptable and expected way to behave when interacting with others. We saw this in the story of Sally who, despite all of her biological systems alerting her to danger, chose to ignore those alarms in favour of social etiquette. The door ajar, the man in the locked stairwell, the man's voice that she didn't like and his insistence on helping all alerting her to danger, she did not want to be rude. After all, this nice man was simply trying to help, and society tells us to be nice in reply. In doing so we ignore the very thing that, in some situations, just might save your life.

Sometimes we know what to do, we just choose not to.

~ 5 ~

Mr J was a 37-year-old teacher who experienced a period of ill mental health and had accessed his income protection, an area where I do a lot of my work. He was referred to me by the insurance company. At the time of the referral, Mr J was in crisis. The most fundamental problem being, he was homeless, he was literally hanging on the second rung of Maslow's Hierarchy of Needs (see below), and I was asked to initially work with him to find accommodation and then to see if I could assist him with his rehabilitation and eventual return to work.

Maslow original (1943, 1954) Hierarchy of Needs stated that people are motivated to achieve certain needs and that some needs take precedence over others. Our most basic need is for physical survival, and this will be the first thing that motivates our behaviour. Once that level is fulfilled the next level up is what motivates us, and so on.

In short, the five rungs of Maslow's hierarchical ladder are:

1. Physiological Needs – these are biological requirements for human survival, e.g., air, food, drink, shelter, clothing, warmth, sex, sleep.

If these needs are not satisfied, the human body cannot function optimally. Maslow considered physiological needs the most important as all the other needs become secondary until these needs are met.

2. Safety Needs – once an individual's physiological needs are satisfied, the needs for security and safety become salient. People want to experience order, predictability and control in their lives. These needs can be fulfilled by the family and society (e.g., police, schools, business and medical care).

For example, emotional security, financial security (e.g., employment, social welfare), law and order, freedom from fear, social stability, property, health and wellbeing (e.g., safety against accidents and injury).

3. Love And Belongingness – after physiological and safety needs have been fulfilled, the third level of human needs is social and involves feelings of belongingness. Belongingness refers to a human emotional need for interpersonal relationships, affiliating, connectedness, and being part of a group.

Examples of belongingness needs include friendship, intimacy, trust, and acceptance, receiving and giving affection, and love.

4. Esteem needs are the fourth level in Maslow's hierarchy and include self-worth, accomplishment, and respect. Maslow classified esteem needs into two categories: (i) esteem for oneself (dignity, achievement, mastery, independence), and (ii) the desire for reputation or respect from others (e.g., status, prestige).

Maslow indicated that the need for respect or reputation is most important for children and adolescents and precedes real self-esteem or dignity.

5. Self-Actualisation needs are the highest level in Maslow's hierarchy and refer to the realisation of a person's potential, self-fulfilment, seeking personal growth and peak experiences. Maslow (1943) describes this level as the desire to accomplish everything that one can, to become the most that one can be.

More modern thinkers such as Tony Robbins have updated

the hierarchy to encompass more contemporary situations. Robbins' hierarchy works somewhat differently to Maslow. First, Robbins opines that there are six human needs (not five) and that they are more a continuum that you are spread across, but the theory is still the same.

1. **Certainty**: assurance you can avoid pain and gain pleasure
2. **Uncertainty/Variety**: the need for the unknown, change, new stimuli
3. **Significance**: feeling unique, important, special or needed
4. **Connection/Love**: a strong feeling of closeness or union with someone or something
5. **Growth**: an expansion of capacity, capability or understanding
6. **Contribution**: a sense of service and focus on helping, giving to and supporting others

Personally, I think that Robbins 'human needs' are more relevant now, particular with the advent of social media. But that is a whole other discussion. Back to Mr J.

For our initial meeting, Mr J arrived on time. He was dressed in shorts and a t-shirt appropriate to the meeting and carried a towel which he used to remove sweat after walking to the meeting location. After introducing himself, Mr J explained to me that his medication caused him to sweat profusely.

Throughout the assessment, Mr J fidgeted with his hands and/or spoke with his hands, making grand gestures. On three occasions Mr J became teary when discussing the separation of his marriage and the relocation of his wife and two children to another country.

On several occasions throughout the discussion and increasingly toward the end of the meeting when the parties began to set goals for the next few days, Mr J self-encouraged, making statements like *'you can do this'* to himself or *'I can do this'*. This, in my experience, is common in people with low self-esteem. They make statements like this in an effort to convince themselves that they are in control. More so at times when control has been lost.

At other times throughout the assessment, Mr J became anxious and appeared to have some moments of realisation with regard to the reality of the position he found himself in, without accommodation and with no employment.

Mr J's second 'light bulb' moment appeared to come when I worked through a raw budget with him. Prior to his wife leaving, she had been charged with management of the family finances. Based on his current income from his income protection, I worked through the cost of living with the outcome showing Mr J would have limited to no surplus income at the end of each month.

On the bright side, the sale of Mr J's family home had left him with some money in the bank after distribution of his ex-wife's share and we were able to secure accommodation for a six-month period, pre-paid, to start the rehabilitation process.

At the time of initial assessment, Mr J reported a wild chronology leading up to and since onset of his diagnosed bipolar disorder. A disorder characterised by extreme shifts in mood. Symptoms can include an extremely elevated mood called mania. They can also include episodes of depression.

Bipolar disorder is also known as bipolar disease or manic depression. People with bipolar disorder may have trouble managing every-day life tasks at school or work or maintaining relationships. There's no cure, but there are many treatment options available that can help manage the symptoms.

Some facts about bipolar disorder. Bipolar disorder isn't a rare brain disorder. In fact, 2.8% of adults have been diagnosed with it. The average age when people with bipolar disorder begin to show symptoms is 25 years of age. Depression caused by bipolar disorder lasts at least two weeks. A high (manic) episode can last for several days or weeks. Some people will experience episodes of changes in mood several times a year, while others may experience them only rarely.

According to Mr J approximately four years before we met, he began to experience symptoms of general anxiety. He reported that he attempted to implement strategies – breathing, mindfulness – but could not get them to embed and he became depressed. His symptoms continued for approximately two years until he had his first psychotic episode in 2016; a period of mania. Mr J was admitted to a psychiatric hospital for a period. Once he stabilised, he was diagnosed with bipolar disorder and prescribed an anti-psychotic and an antidepressant.

At the time he was living with his wife and two young sons aged two and four. He reported that he took six months off work until December 2016 and, due to his employment as a school teacher, was required to undergo a Fitness for Work Assessment by the Department of Education before being allowed to teach again.

He reported that at this time he continued to see a psychologist for treatment, techniques to manage his symptoms and behaviour and prevent onset, his general practitioner for general health, and a psychiatrist. Psychiatrists are required for the prescription of medication. A Psychologist and/or a GP cannot prescribe anti-psychotics and/or diagnose a psychiatric condition. He reported also seeing an independent psychiatrist in February 2017 related to his ability to return to work.

Mr J attempted a return to work on reduced hours and duties, two days weekly in February 2017. The intended plan to increase to four days weekly in Semester 2 and with the goal of returning to full pre-condition hours and duties in Semester 3.

He reported that, in his opinion, the return to work was not structured enough, advising that the principal provided too much latitude which validated his manic or depressive thought patterns. Mr J reported completing Semester 2 and having a second psychotic episode during the break. Sitting there talking with me he was able to recognise the trigger for both psychotic episodes as report writing. He told me that when it came to report writing he felt overwhelmed by the magnitude (30+ reports) of the task. The principal had tried to assist with provision of someone that could type whilst he dictated; however, this meant he had to process his thinking inside his head and this contributed to an increase in anxiety.

Mr J's second psychotic episode involved a number of "domestic incidents". He would not elaborate but went on to report that the incidents resulted in him being admitted to a psychiatric hospital for several days. According to Mr J, it was during this period of admittance that the psychiatric team recommended a change of diagnosis to Borderline Personality Disorder (BPD). Borderline Personality Disorder is a mental health disorder that impacts the way you think and feel about yourself and others, causing problems functioning in everyday life. It includes self-image issues, difficulty managing emotions and behaviour, and a pattern of unstable relationships.

With BPD, you have an intense fear of abandonment or instability, and you may have difficulty tolerating being alone. Yet inappropriate anger, impulsiveness and frequent mood swings may push others away, even though you want to have loving and lasting relationships. Borderline Personality Disorder usually begins by early adulthood. The condition seems to be worse in young adulthood and may gradually get better with age.

Mr J told me that not long after provision of this diagnosis he was released from hospital and moved in with his parents. Things were beginning to spiral out of control. He reported that he felt he was released without support, and told me that whilst the Crisis Assessment Team (CAT) would check in on him regularly, he had been told to find a suitable psychiatrist that could assist with the new diagnosis. According to Mr J, he approached several facilities and was declined services because "his diagnosis was too complex".

It was during this period that his family relationship fractured, and he went through a period of drug taking (cocaine and

Ice). Mr J told me that he used the drugs for two main reasons:
1) To keep going at what he felt was a high functioning rate.
2) Maintain happiness.

He also reported a history of pleasure-seeking by shopping, which resulted in some family financial difficulties. In August 2017, Mr J made attempts to reconcile with his wife, which failed, and she moved with their two children to another country.

Mr J reported moving back into the family home and commenced regular attendance at an outpatient psychiatric clinic under the care of the in-house psychiatrist once a week, which at the time of writing this book, continues today albeit now twice weekly. Mr J attends to continue a Dialectical Behaviour Therapy (DBT) program that is a structured outpatient treatment developed by Dr Marsha Linehan for the treatment of borderline personality disorder (BPD).

Dialectical behaviour therapy is based on cognitive-behavioural principles and is currently the only empirically supported treatment for BPD. Randomised controlled trials have shown the efficacy of DBT not only in BPD but also in other psychiatric disorders such as substance use disorders, mood disorders, post-traumatic stress disorder, and eating disorders.

Traditional DBT is structured into four components, including skills training group, individual psychotherapy, telephone consultation, and therapist consultation team. These components work together to teach behavioural skills that target common symptoms of BPD, including an unstable sense of self, chaotic relationships, fear of abandonment, emotional lability, and impulsivity such as self-injurious behaviours. The skills include mindfulness, interpersonal effectiveness, emotion regulation, and distress tolerance. Given the often-comorbid psychiatric symptoms with BPD in patients participating in DBT, psychopharmacologic interventions are also considered appropriate adjunctive care.

The second attendance at the clinic was for a session with the psychiatrist. Mr J reported relying on the clinic for continued functionality. He also told me that he and his wife had agreed to sell the family home. Mr J received no support from her during this process and told me that he had literally sold and moved their possessions on his own. He was living in an Air B&B, and advised that all the family furniture and belongings were in storage.

For several months Mr J and I worked together to establish routine and solve some of the other issues that had been manufactured during his periods of psychosis. He had purchased a vehicle and not paid any money for it, accumulating a debt exceeding $50,000, and the country his wife had moved to was chasing him for child support.

Mr J made great progress and started to resolve a lot of the issues that had mounted up in recent times. He was starting to see some light, but when his wedding anniversary and the birthday of one of his children (very close together) came around, he spiralled and went missing for several days.

Uncontactable for seven days, I eventually had to request a welfare check by police. The police went to his house and found him safe – severely depressed and suicidal, but safe. I thought they would walk in on a body for sure. We got him admitted again and he spent the next several months as an inpatient.

Mr J again worked hard and re-joined the world some four months after being admitted. He was able to travel to see his family and with the help of his psychiatrist, we were able to help him shape a relationship with his ex-wife to a point where Mr J planned to move to the same country in order to have a relationship with his children.

He had an even bigger problem looming, however. Whilst we had solved a lot of his issues, his Income Protection Policy was a two-year policy and due to expire in two months' time. This would leave him with no income and ability to live. His car issue remained unresolved, and his pre-paid accommodation would expire at the same time that his income protection ran out.

I met with Mr J to plan and implement the next phase of his recovery: a return to work. This would facilitate an income where he would be able to pay for accommodation and, as we as occupational therapists believe and studies have shown, Mr J would regain a sense of wellbeing as he achieved personal accountability again and was able to contribute to society.

In speaking with Mr J, he showed insight. He was able to tell me that all he needed to do was register for casual relief teacher (CRT). He could use the money from the sale of the family home to buy new accommodation. He could work with the car loan company to pay off the loan over time, and he could make regular trips to see his children. Mr J could see the required action. His intuition told him what he needed to do, but again, like Sally, he was choosing to ignore the biological signals that would get him out of trouble for favour of procrastination.

This, unfortunately, is common in people with mental illness. They know what to do. And if, like Sally, they just listened to the intuitive voice (not psychotic voices) inside them telling them what to do to get out of trouble, they might just be all right. The pattern, however, seems to be that their brain's chemical make-up at the time causes them to procrastinate. Things escalate and the trouble only worsens. Somewhere in this journey, in their mind, the trouble becomes insurmountable and the intuitive voice changes to: the thing to do now is kill yourself. And so many people do, as you learned in Chapter 1 – My Life.

I am pleased to say this was not the case with Mr J. He continued to work with me, his psychiatrist and the team at the clinic. He was able to re-build enough to re-establish his life. I still see him from time to time and each visit he gives me a big hug. He is a big unit, so his hugs damn near crush you, but they also pass on his gratitude for my help in his time of crisis. For housing him and keeping him safe from himself until he could get back on his feet.

I still tell him what I tell all the people I work with: you know what to do. Even if you can't consciously manifest a plan, deep down inside you, your years of experience, years of learning, years of assessing stimulus to determine the threats and deciding whether to fight or flee will tell you what you need to know. You just need to listen to the voice early and follow your intuition, follow your heart. It is your protector. It has protected people for generations, and it will protect you if you listen and if you hear before your problems are insurmountable.

So, Bridge Two of your journey to transforming your life is to follow your intuition. Think about all those times you haven't followed your heart. You may regret it now. I personally don't have many regrets, but I chose to ignore my heart twice in my life and in doing so I made two monumental, life-changing decisions that I could never take back nor change. It caused me a lot of stress and anger. It took me a long time to learn to live with those decisions. There was certainly no going back. I would estimate it took me the best part of ten years to recover and that's a long time to be thinking about something you can do nothing about. That is what can happen. Just like Mr J, you can become so all-consumed by the mistake that you forget to live.

Transforming your life is all about listening to what you want out of it, ignoring what other people want for you, and going after your dream. Think about what you wanted to be growing up. Are you doing it? If not, why not? Like me, have you turned an irreversible corner and struggled or are struggling to get over it? Or did you follow societal pressure and do what others expected? Maybe it is a mixture of all of the above.

No matter where you are at in your life, no matter what has happened, it is not too late. If you first follow your intuition and then the rest of the advice in this book, then you will recover! You will bounce back! Your life will be transformed.

So, before we venture on to Bridge Three I want you to do a little activity. I want you to write a list of all the things you want to do or achieve in your life. I want you to write these in five key areas:

1) **Life Goals**: these are the things you really want to do before you kick the bucket. Your bucket list.

2) **Business/Employment Goals**: the things you want to achieve in your business and/or career.

3) **Toys**: things you want to have in your life; e.g., car, skis, anything.

4) **Relationship Goals**: what you want in a relationship; and

5) **Contribution Goals**: how you want to contribute to the world. This might be by financial donation, volunteering, or any other way you can give back.

Go on, write them out. When you have, come back.

Well done! You now have the start of your Transformation plan! I'll help you to develop a strategy for achievement in future chapters. It's time now to keep reading.

In the Ownership chapter we learned that all the people I have worked with, first had to own their circumstance, the decisions they made to put themselves in that place (no matter how small) and their contribution to that event. In this chapter we have learned that you know what you want, you just need to be prepared to go after it. You just need to follow your heart, or your bliss as Joseph Campbell would have it. You will learn more about him in the final chapter.

In the next chapter, you will learn what it takes to cross the next bridge and how to become comfortable with making change.

Chapter 4

CHANGE

You are the creator of your life not the manager of your circumstance.

– Tony Robbins

~ 1 ~

You could cut the air with a knife. The delivery as impactful as always and is the result of 20 years of living it. The sense of the experience that the audience gets from Alan's story means that each one of them can feel the pain, the frustration, the anger and the pride. Now one of the most sought-after public speakers on the circuit, Alan never misses a moment to make his message clear. A message I am sure he would rather not be the one to deliver. One that he would not have to deliver if not for that one day in September 1999.

He's come a long way since 30 September 1999. A day Alan will never forget, nor his wife.... his work colleagues and the now thousands of people that Alan has spoken in front of.

I am now sitting in the audience after one of his talks to a group of employees about workplace safety. There is no doubt that this crowd has understood the message and been sobered by Alan's description of his experience. At the same time, there is an atmosphere of appreciation. No one in the room will ever fully grasp what Alan has just articulated, but they appreciate his strength, his grit, his ability to accept change and his zest to just get on with life.

I remember when I first met Alan. I was the state manager for the National Safety Council of Australia (NSCA). He was introduced to me by my then business development manager as a person we should have speak at one of our many member breakfasts. That was 10 years ago now and I have been privileged to witness firsthand Alan's phoenix-like recovery and return to the living.

As a young fella, I was always blown away by the human body's ability to take punishment and bounce back. To heal and to surprise people. Its fragility and its hardiness. We truly are an amazing organism. What the human body must do to become human and what it must do to maintain life for, in a large percentage of cases, 80-plus years. It is one fucking amazing thing – don't ever doubt that. And that is why I became an occupational therapist. I just had to get amongst it. And as I explained in the opening chapter, I have certainly given it a good nudge.

I never actually worked with Alan in the rehabilitation sense, other than to have him speak at several of our functions but I've been honoured to work with thousands of people with equally catastrophic injuries and conditions. Some of them you have and will read about in this book. Some of them followed what I articulate in these pages and now live fantastic new lives. Some couldn't get out of their own heads to clear a path to freedom, and they remain in their prison. For the time being, these people have given up on themselves. They have been unable to cross the bridge and move forward. They have lost their way and may not return. I can only help people so far. It is you who needs to do the hard work. Rest assured, if you need help and are willing to follow the path I propose in this book, then you can and will transform your life, and I will never give up on you.

Alan could have so easily given up. If you speak with him he will tell you that there were plenty of occasions when he thought about it. One of those being not long before I met him. He didn't give up though, and as tough as the times got, it was his sheer fortitude and, he will tell you, the love and support of his wife that got him through it.

That is why his story is the ideal story for this book. After his accident, Alan went through everything this book talks about. He knew what he needed to do and avoided doing it until he was able to own his situation. He followed the intuitive voice to help him move forward, he focused and lost focus, he changed, and he did it with self-resilience, tapping into his relationships and networks to win in life. Alan is the epitome of Transformation.

To write this book I have spent hours with Alan talking about the last 20 years. He can't believe it has been that long. Alan still remembers in detail the day in question. That is why he can speak so genuinely about it. He remembers how many times he had done the job and the vivid details on a minute-by-minute basis. I guess with that sort of trauma, your mind either shuts it out or etches it into the filing cabinet that is memory. The latter being the case for Alan.

~ 2 ~

It was just another day for Alan Newey, a then 35-year-old crane driver/plant operator at a Melbourne-based fertiliser plant. He got up at his usual time and left the house at 7am. At 7.20am he met his friend and work colleague at the gate. These two guys were more than just colleagues, they were friends, and the usual jibes passed amongst them as they started the workday.

There were two main jobs that these men shared between them. The first in the control room monitoring plant operation and the second in the tower undertaking crane operation and monitoring the belts on the conveyor.

Alan was scheduled to be in the control room that day, but for whatever reason the two swapped roles. This wasn't unusual. They swapped all the time.

Alan climbed the 30ft tower to the top of the plant. Something he had done four thousand, five hundred and eighty-six times before. Once in the tower he began the usual checks and found that once again the belts had slipped to the side on the conveyor. This was not uncommon and something that might happen two or three times each day. Moisture builds up on the rollers causing the belts to slip sideways.

The fix was easy. Take the 'Zelite' (a drying dust) and throw it between the rollers. The belt would usually grab and re-centre. As articulated, this was something Alan had done at least four thousand, five hundred and eighty-six times, so he thought nothing of it.

Picking up the Zelite, he began to throw the dust. According to Alan, whilst the belt was moving back to the centre, it was not moving far enough. When this occurred, the next step was to throw dust into the main drive. As he began to do so, he remembers hearing a bang and not long after hearing a knocking in the rollers, like something was going around inside them. Alan tells me that he thought nothing of it but walked up and down the belt looking for the noise.

Now you need to understand that Alan is a laidback sort of dude and loves a joke. It is easy to imagine him taking a casual approach to a catastrophic situation. Particularly when involving himself.

Alan tells me that when unable to find the noise he went to scratch his head and found his arm to be no longer there. Alan says there was no pain. He remembers simply thinking, *I'm in trouble here.*

So, what actually happened? Investigators surmise and, based on the evidence, Alan got too close to the rollers and his hand was caught. No shit! This is the WOW bit though. Moving at breakneck speed, he was picked up, thrown around a nearby pole where the force ripped his arm off and rotated his entire rib cage to the side. He had then been put back in the almost exact spot where his arm had been caught. The extreme violence and speed of the incident, despite being lifted off his feet, thrown around the pole and back onto the platform, Alan's brain could not register that anything had occurred. Now do you see why I love injury management, occupational therapy and the human body!

But why does this happen? Well, it is a normal thing that the person involved in a major or catastrophic accident doesn't remember the moment of the accident or right after. That's because the mind and the body enter a more alert but also more stressed state, particularly in major incidents, with trade-offs that can save your life, but harm your mind's memory-making abilities.

Basically, the brain is focused on its fight or flight response. The memory-making function takes a back seat to look for a way to escape the impending trauma. Further, the adrenaline that's generated during a traumatic event can block any information that isn't needed for someone to survive in the moment. Pretty cool, eh?

Now I can't say for sure, but knowing Alan, I feel that even at this time, he remained calm. He will tell you there was some panic, but he tells me that he ran down the platform, climbed, one-handed down the 30ft ladder and started running across the yard yelling for help. Alan's friend and colleague was first on scene. Running out from the control room, he apparently latched onto the stump, attempting to stop the bleeding and promptly passed out. Alan now had no choice but to carry him the remaining fifty metres to first aid.

Once there, the first aid boys began to work on him. Alan was fully conscious throughout. He was stabilised and readied for transport to hospital whilst maintenance cut his detached arm out of the machinery.

Fortuitously for Alan, Professor Wayne Morrison, plastics and reconstruction specialist was on call that day. Overall, he attempted to re-attach Alan's arm five times over a four-week period. Performing microscopic surgery, reuniting vessels and muscles with precision and skill beyond comprehension. But it was not enough. Alan's arm turned septic and threatened to poison his entire body. With an estimated two hours to live, Alan's wife was forced to sign consent for the arm to be permanently and completely amputated. In total, Alan bled and had replaced twenty-four litres of blood. Don't forget to donate when you can.

Alan being Alan though, was awake and watching the Bledisloe Cup (Australia v New Zealand in Rugby Union) two hours after the surgery. Unusually, Australia won that year and retained the cup for a second year in a row. I digress, but as a New Zealander it is the ultimate trans-Tasman battle.

Still, there was a hard road ahead. Alan tells me that he spent the next ten days on drugs and he doesn't remember much. During his time in hospital, he endured painful skin graphs from his thigh for application to the stump. At one stage his shoulder locked with the remaining muscles and tendons adhering to the bone requiring an excruciating procedure where the nurses held Alan down and ripped them apart. According to Alan, it was so painful that if he had the choice, he would rather have his arm ripped off again. Then to top it all off after one skin graph and with an open and raw wound on his thigh, his wife came and sat on his lap – it was time for her to leave the hospital.

Alan tells me that it took three-months before he would recognise that the arm was not there. He wouldn't look at the arm and he didn't want to leave the hospital. The hospital was a safe place. The accident had happened outside the hospital, so why would you want to go out there? In addition, whilst in hospital he was the responsibility of the staff. Outside it was his responsibility and he didn't want to burden his wife with that.

It is amazing how much we take for granted. It is not until something happens that things become precious. I remember when I was a stupid young man, only slightly less stupid than I am now. I punched a brick wall in a moment of impetuosity and fractured some bones in my dominant hand. Stupid, I know! In a cast for six-weeks I had to learn how to wipe my backside with my left hand. Try it! It's not easy.

Only temporary for me, this was a permanent challenge for Alan. New ways to wash your hair, dress, butter toast and many more of the things we find easy with two hands. It is not surprising that deep-seated depression set in.

Why me? I must have done something bad for this to have happened! All rattling round in Alan's head, and an overwhelming need to hide from the public. By hiding he could not be the victim, have looks of pity flashed in his direction or be judged by the scathing and less-than-understanding human race. Alan was in a dark place for quite some time.

Enter, Mrs Cathy Newey. This woman should have been an occupational therapist. According to Alan, she provided him an ultimatum of one-week to get off the couch. Get up and moving or I leave; simple.

Now Mrs Newey is a beautiful and tough woman. She is someone you want on your side when the shit is going down. So, Alan did the only thing he could do. He got off his arse. Like a military general, Mrs Newey commanded her sorry-for-himself man. She made him walk the streets daily and do the dishes by hand, by himself, even though they had a dishwasher. What a hard arse! Ant Middleton from SAS, you're a wimp.

She was not being hard though. She simply was and remains his biggest fan and the only person that could have gotten Alan out of his funk. Frankly, I am a bit of a fan of her myself. I love a good, kick your arse to get you motivated story and this one is a pearler. In my experience, it is a special bond that can get the best out of people in these times and Alan and Mrs Newey have that bond.

Whilst up and moving, there remained two big problems. Very common when people are injured. Particularly when that injury is a game-changer, a maiming that cannot be recovered from without big change to you and transformation of your life.

The first common problem is an inability to ask for help. We humans are a weird bunch! We maintain a false belief throughout life that we are the best and that no one can do it better than us. This belief stays, even when we are in big trouble and sometimes our own doggedness stops us from moving on. For Alan, he didn't want to give up and say that he needed help. He ordered shoelaces from America that can be done up with one hand and refused to let any task stop him.

Now this is good when it comes to rehabilitation and returning to the living after you have had your arm ripped off. But not so good when you won't listen to people who can make life easier or when you are putting yourself in harm's way. When your anger is becoming overwhelming and the dark hoody of depression creeps over you. The people around you can see the problem but you're just too close to it. Alan tells me it took a long time to own his situation, accept help, and even now he still has trouble.

The second problem is drug addiction. As I am sure you will understand, having your arm ripped off is likely one hell of a painful experience. For those of us fortunate enough to never know, we can get barely a glimpse of what it might be like from the stories of those unfortunate enough to have experienced the loss of a limb. Phantom pains, unscratchable itches and the feeling like the limb is still there. All caused by neurons firing, giving the brain false messages.

A quick explanation of this is that phantom pain typically occurs soon after limb loss. It can take three to six months for a wound to heal after amputation. Rarely, the pain comes on months or years later. Experts believe phantom pain results from a mix-up in nervous system signals, specifically between the spinal cord and brain. When a body part is amputated, the nerve connections from the periphery to the brain remain in place. The brain can misinterpret the information it's receiving or process the signals as the sensation of pain, even if the amputated portion has since been removed.

For Alan, his pain was managed by a high level of prescription medication. Some of the big ones like morphine included. For two years he lived in a fog of drug-assisted pain relief. Unable to fully function. Slow thought, short-term memory loss, fatigue, an inability to focus, and a loss of insight into the future, your behaviour, and the affect you are having on those around you. According to Alan it was a near constant thought about drugs and numbing the pain. Not stopping for a minute. His safe place until in 2001, when he recognised a need to shed his prescription-based armour and face reality. Alan needed a pain clinic.

The pain clinic guaranteed a 10% reduction in reliance on medication in ten days. The class focussed on coping without meds. How do they do it? Well, according to Alan, he was handed a golf club (putter) and a golf ball and told to putt the ball around the halls of the hospital. Easy right? Now imagine doing it in a backless hospital gown. Your focus is temporarily directed to your dignity and away from your pain.

It took Alan eleven minutes and twenty-three seconds to putt the hospital course, and for eleven minutes and twenty-three seconds Alan did not think about pain or medication at all. By gradually growing this period of distraction, he was able to come completely off medication and take one of the most important steps in recovering from anything: owning his situation. He realised he needed to talk about it.

As discussed in Chapter 2, by owning your situation and talking about it, you switch from a victim of circumstance to life creator. It is not until you own your situation and the fact that you contributed to your circumstance, that you can transform your life using the other steps I espouse in the pages of this book. It is not until you reach this point that you will have a chance of recovery and living a whole and fulfilling life like Alan.

Now I must make it clear here, my experiences in rehabilitation are not exclusive to physical injury. Mental health problems are the fastest growing issue in the civilised world as you read in the stats at the start of this book. I have my opinion as to why this is, and the people working in the depths of this industry have theirs. This book is not about cause, it's about recovery, building resilience and building the life you want in any circumstance. So, we won't go into my thoughts on this. I'll save that for my second book.

This book does not just relate to injury (physical or mental) recovery either. My aim is to espouse a strategy for transformation in any circumstance. Your life may have taken an unexpected turn; a divorce or death of a loved one. You may not like your life, but don't know how to make the changes necessary to transform it. Whatever your circumstance, I want to pass on the strategies of the people who know. The people that have overcome adversity to create the life they have always dreamt about, and live transformed.

~ 3 ~

At the time of the initial assessment, Peter reported the following:

In the months leading up to June 2016, he began to struggle with his vision. He reported losing an ability to see text on a computer screen and in documents, and compensated by printing things out in extremely large fonts and on A3 paper, but the problem continued to worsen.

In Peter's words, "like most males, I left it thinking it would get better". He reported that his colleagues at work started to notice his changed work patterns and he finally sought medical attention in late September 2016.

The initial medical assessment was with his GP, who referred him to an eye specialist. According to Peter, he underwent a barrage of tests and was told that he was legally blind. An offical diagnosis of tunnel vision and optic atrophy.

Optic atrophy is a condition that affects the optic nerve, which carries impulses from the eye to the brain. (Atrophy means to waste away or deteriorate.)

Optic atrophy is not a disease, but rather a sign of a potentially more serious condition. Optic atrophy results from damage to the optic nerve from many different kinds of pathologies. The condition can cause problems with vision, including blindness.

The cause in its basic form is that something is interfering with the optic nerve's ability to transmit impulses to the brain, and can come from numerous factors, including, but not limited to:

- Glaucoma.
- Stroke of the optic nerve, known as anterior ischemic optic neuropathy.
- A tumor that is pressing on the optic nerve.
- Optic neuritis, an inflammation (swelling) of the optic nerve caused by multiple sclerosis.
- A hereditary condition in which the person experiences loss of vision first in one eye, and then in the other (known as Leber's hereditary optic neuropathy).
- Improper formation of the optic nerve, which is a congenital problem (the person is born with it).

In Peter's case the cause was a combination of hereditary factors and congenital issues.

Soon after the diagnosis, Peter parted ways with his employer and his driver's licence was cancelled. He reported having been seeing a psychologist who, when I first met Peter, he had not seen for six weeks.

Peter had recently made attempts to change career by starting a Bachelors Degree in Health Science (Myopathy). He reported having to pull out of the course because of light sensitivity to the fluroescent lights in the classrooms.

He was engaged with another occupational therapist who had conducted a home assessment and was working with him to lay out his home in a functional manner that would prevent Peter from running into furniture etc. Yes, this is one of the roles of an OT in the community sector. In addition, the OT had prescribed and obtained some assistive equipment which included an electronic reader that enlarges documents etc., to a size that allows Peter to see the item. Peter also reported having implemented some compensatory techniques such as taking photos of the train station departures board on his phone so he could enlarge and see the list when necessary.

Peter was also working with Guide Dogs Victoria. He had undergone an initial review and was working through the process of being allocated an assistance canine. Peter's treating practitioners were unable to provide a prognosis. They were unsure if his eyesight would deteriorate further. All they knew was that his condition is rare, and his blood had been taken and sent to Perth for analysis.

Whilst Peter presented well, he was clearly struggling with this change. He refused to use a cane when walking, which had resulted in some painful falls and he was refusing to speak with the psychologist. For Peter, though, it was not a case of refusing to own the problem like our friend from Chapter Two, it was a refusal to give up his way of life and accommodate (remember the process) his new situation. A refusal to change.

Now Peter and I worked together for some time and formed a great relationship. Over time his eyesight deteriorated further, but before it did, I managed to help him finish his training as a myotherapist and open his own practice. To my knowledge he continues to practise in the northern suburbs of Melbourne, Australia, and after he and I worked to help him cross the Bridge of Change, he is thriving in the community, living a fulfilling life, and is married with two kids. He himself admits that until he embraced the change, his life was very unfulfilled but once he did accept the change life vastly transformed.

~ 4 ~

Back to Alan. As we can see with Peter, when he accepted the change of lifestyle and embraced his new way of living his life transformed to one of enjoyment and positivity. The same occurred for Alan. Now owning his situation, Alan was able to start considering what was next for him. He felt a calling to injury prevention, but he didn't really know how to get there or what it might look like.

He initially started to look for work but experienced rejection after rejection and this, of course, fed into a negative mind space which caused Alan to withdraw and not want to put himself out there. Eventually he applied for a role at Bunnings within a group of 100 applicants. Alan was sure his limitation would be seen as a good reason not to be hired. The opposite occurred. Alan met the Managing Director who told him that he could not see a limitation and offered him a job.

Initially, Alan did not want the job. In his head he had not yet accepted how he presented to others and until he could accept this in his own mind, it would be difficult. Alan reluctantly accepted the role and 10 years later he was still working there. Alan's confidence and ability to be around people again just grew from there.

Now I am big on the phrase, 'where your focus goes, energy flows', as you will see in the next chapter. Part of Alan's role with Bunnings was to talk to staff about workplace safety. Little did Alan know that his big break would come from this very thing. Somehow, Alan's advocacy for workplace safety was noticed and he was invited to speak about his experience and the value of safety in the workplace for the Department of Justice, Prisons.

Now you need to be aware that this offer coincided with a massive change in workplace cultural right across Australia (about 2007). Before now, workplace safety was not really a thing. Whilst companies acknowledged a duty of care for their workers, they were not really focused on prevention. More an ambulance at the bottom of the cliff scenario. Workcover was seen with a high level of negative stigma. Most people on Workcover were considered malingering. Genuine injury or not. And mental health was only just becoming something other than a bunch of hippies on a yoga camp. So in some way you could say that Alan was in the forefront, a pioneer of sorts, for the advocacy of workplace safety and prevention. Zero harm.

Alan admits that it as with some reluctancy that he agreed to present. He likened it to putting the ball around the hospital. He felt completely exposed. Nevertheless, the speech was well received, and word started to spread about Alan's charismatic, real life experience and its hard-hitting uptake from audiences. Since this first presentation Alan has started his own business 'Chat Safety' and has presented to most of Australia's big, small to medium, and large organisations. He has presented on a range of topics including his workplace accident, hospital to rehabilitation, the effect on family and friends, coping with a workplace injury, Worksafe investigations, light at the end of the tunnel, and complacency and his favourite message to ALL employers and employees. Feel free to visit his website www.chatsafety.com.au to view a full list. He has truly established a successful business in the space that his intuition told him was his calling.

Now I have given you the condensed version of Alan's story; there is a lot of heartache, hard times and hard work that is not discussed in Alan's story. It certainly has not been a case where Alan owned his role in the incident, decided what he had to do next and made the change. There were two more bridges that he needed to cross to make this success story a reality. We are going to talk about the Fourth Bridge in a moment but before we do, here are some things to consider when adapting your mindset on change.

~ 5 ~

Change is a real and continuous part of life, especially in the hectic world we live in today. Not only is everything around you changing, but you change as well. The problem is many of us will initially refuse to accept, and even reject it. Just as we saw with Mike in Chapter Two and Peter and Alan in this chapter.

Change can be terrifying and complicated, but change is often a good thing and can be so worth embracing. Also, as we have seen in the pages to date, we need to remember that not all change feels good. If we can handle it and look at it in the right way, growth as well as good outcomes can come from accepting change.

Here are some reasons why embracing change can transform your life.

1. **Education:** Change allows you to learn new things you normally wouldn't have learned with old ways. Even if the change involves failure, oftentimes a lot more can be learned from failure than success. Learning doesn't just stop at school. It's a lifelong process. The more we seek out change and new experiences, the more learning opportunities are presented to us. Change can force you to look at things in a new light and challenge your current beliefs, values, and knowledge. It can allow you to learn new ideas,

skills, viewpoints, and information. You can also learn and discover new things about yourself.

2. **Adaptability:** Accepting and embracing change allows you to adapt better to change and become more flexible. Change can be a lot harder on someone when they resist and reject it. Accepting change makes dealing with change a lot easier. The more we deal with change, the more used to it we become, and the easier it becomes to deal with it. Rigidity and resistance can cause unnecessary stress and blind us from the good that new situations, environments, and people can bring.

3. **Opportunities And Possibilities:** As we have seen from our heroes to date, change can open many doors and opportunities that normally wouldn't have been there without said change. Change makes many things possible. It can allow you to meet new people, enjoy new experiences, develop new skills and ideas, learn new knowledge and information, and achieve great feats. Change can help you transform and have breakthroughs. You'll never know what you can become and what can happen until you do. The possibilities with change become endless.

4. **Improvement:** Improvement is impossible without change. Change is necessary for improvement, growth, and development to take place. Change doesn't have to be drastic or sudden either; it can be slow and steady for improvement and growth to happen. Seeking and embracing change not only ensures you keep up with the times and stay up to date, but also allows you to get ahead. Change allows for progress.

5. **Greatness:** Greatness is more likely when you embrace

change. It's easier to remain stagnant and comfortable when you are 'good', but you miss the potential and opportunity of becoming great whether it be with your job, your relationships, or any skill or hobby you pursue.

Many people reject change because they claim to be happy already, but with change, they have the potential to become happier. Many of us don't know what we're missing because we are okay with where we are. Lack of change and resistance to change makes it a lot easier to settle.

6. **Courage:** When you are openly embracing change in life, it reduces and can eliminate the fears that can come with change. When change pushes us out of our comfort zone, courage grows. We can slowly but surely overcome our fears by embracing the change that comes from facing those fears. And yes, those fears can include the fear of change itself. Fear is an illusion in our minds that only stops us from seeking and achieving greater things in life.

7. **Resilience:** – Acceptance of change makes us more resilient. Resilience makes us stronger and more capable of dealing with life's difficulties. You learn that when there's a change in your life, however big it may be, that it's not the end of the world and you'll get through it, probably even better than before. We're more equipped and efficacious with what life throws at us because of the changes we've dealt with before. Without change, you can never know your strengths and of what you are truly capable. What we learn about ourselves can be surprising to many of us.

8. **Appreciate Failure And Enjoy Success**: Embracing change allows you to be okay with change, whether it be negative or positive. Some of us can avoid change even if it's positive change and it involves success. Success anxiety is a

very real thing. Many of us can feel more relaxed with less responsibility and less success because we are comfortable with how things are now. Success can be scary and uncomfortable. When we learn to accept change, we can enjoy the success and good things that come with that change and stop self-sabotaging.

9. **Allows You To Be Proactive:** When you accept, embrace, and seek change, it puts the ball in your court and places the direction of your life in your own hands. It allows you to be proactive rather than reactive. You are no longer a victim controlled by outside forces. You make the choices when you embrace change. Only you are responsible for yourself and your life. Implementing changes makes you more likely to reach your goals, develop your character, and live the life you want to live. When you accept change, you stop wasting time and energy complaining about changes that happen around you and instead take the initiative to make your own changes.

10. **Change Can Improve Your Relationships**: Experiencing change can also make you more open-minded and empathetic, which can also improve your relationships with people. When you have more experiences and face difficult and adverse change, you are able to relate to people better and put yourself in their shoes because of the experiences you've had. Change gives you more awareness and different perspectives, insight into other people's experiences and viewpoints that you had never before had. It's harder to relate to people who have limited experiences or haven't faced any of life's challenges. Those people are also going to find it hard to relate to those who have.

11. **You're More Likely To Follow Through With Your Goals:** Even if we have goals and want to reach them, we may

still be resistant to change whether we're aware of it or not. When we embrace change, we're more likely to value our ideas and potential possibilities, and then follow through with them. When we value our ideas and goals, we're more likely to believe in ourselves and our abilities. When we accept change, we're more likely to reach our goals.

To reach our goals we must cross the final two bridges. The next bridge being in my opinion the most important and is our Fourth Bridge – Focus.

Chapter 5

FOCUS

You will never reach your destination if you stop and throw stones at every dog that barks.

– Winston Churchill

~ 1 ~

Just before 9.20 last night, with the court festooned in semi-darkness after almost five hours of epic, see-saw tennis, Rafael Nadal finally prevailed in one of the sport's all-time classics, vanquishing Roger Federer in his attempt to become the first man since the 1880s to win six consecutive Wimbledon championships.

Onlookers were running out of superlatives by the denouement, and not just about the quality of the groundstrokes. It was Wimbledon's longest men's final, perhaps its greatest, a match Nadal finally won 6-4, 6-4, 6-7, 6-7, 9-7.

Federer, who was thrashed by Nadal in straight sets in the French Open final last month, remains the world number one, but the 22-year-old Spaniard may claim the position by the end of the year.

His win gave Spain its second major sporting victory in eight days, its footballers having won Euro 2008. Nadal became the first Spaniard in 42 years to win the Wimbledon men's title, ending Federer's run of 41 unbeaten matches at the All-England club, where he last lost in 2002 ...

Nadal survived a scare in the third set when he slipped and appeared to hurt his right knee. Otherwise, the only other time he was on his back came at the end when Federer hit a forehand into the net. A victorious Nadal clambered up to embrace his family before walking over the commentary box roof to shake hands with the Spanish crown prince and his wife.

Steve Bierley - *The Guardian*, 7 July 2008

Raphael Nadal may be ranked world No. 3 at the time of writing this book but he has held the world No. 1 ranking for a total of 209 weeks and finished the year end world No.1 five times. Known best for his ability on clay (12 French Open titles) he has shown his tennis prowess on multiple surfaces including grass, as the above clip from *The Guardian* aptly describes.

He may be best known in the public eye as the best player on clay or for his lasso forehand, which Andrea Agassi describes as *"just brutal"*. Or even his OCD-type rituals pre-serve. In the tennis circuit and amongst his peers and adversaries on the court however, he is best known for his attitude. Especially his focus.

If you are an avid follower or even just occasional armchair spectator, if you have ever seen Nadal play, there is seldom a time when you could say that he had not given his all in a tennis match. Carlos Moya, former world No.1 and now Nadal's coach, met Nadal for the first time when Nadal was only 12 years old. Moya has said that even then he was astonished at the sheer intensity of Nadal's training.

From the time he broke through in 2003 he has displayed a laser-like-focus like no other. Nadel was once quoted as saying "Endure, put up with whatever comes your way, learn to overcome weakness and pain, push yourself to breaking point but never cave in. If you don't learn that lesson, you'll never succeed as an elite athlete". Or in life for that matter.

He has dominated the head-to-head battles against Federer. Arguably the best player to ever grace the tennis court, winning six of their first seven meetings, two on hard courts. As I write, Nadal has 19 Grand Slam wins to Federer's 20. With Federer close to retirement, Nadal is poised to be the best tennis player ever.

How has he done it? Well, I've already said, FOCUS! What he is best known for amongst his peers. In Nadal's world that means breaking everything down to ensure his concentration is on one point at a time. "I expect to play my best on every point and fight for every point like it is the last one. I don't think if the match is going to be difficult. I just go on court and fight point by point." Nadel said.

~ 2 ~

A similar beast is Connor McGregor, the mad (said with the upmost respect – I certainly would not like to face off with the man) Irishman. Two-time UFC world champion, UFC Feather Weight Belt Holder and UFC Lightweight Belt Holder. The only MMA fighter to hold the two belts in unison.

His superpower? His upmost belief in himself. His insane work ethic and his ability to 'focus on the task at hand'. McGregor and his team will lock themselves away for months in preparation for a fight. This prevents distraction from external sources. McGregor is not infallible. He talks about times of distraction, lack of commitment and reduced motivation. That is part of life. What differentiates the life-creators like McGregor from the circumstance-managers, is the ability to lift and move past these periods of lull.

That is, all they are is a period of lull and that is all they should be. We all need to have a break and recharge. As long as these periods of lull don't become protracted periods of negativity and you can pull yourself out (sometimes requiring help from people like me and, as discussed in the chapter on 'Ownership') to move into something you are truly passionate about, you will be fine. Passion will help you focus.

McGregor's key to focus is his passion. He is not only passionate about his fitness and fighting, but he also loves whiskey. He brought out his own whiskey in 2020 and he loves fashion. He has his own clothing line.

In an interview with the legendary Tony Robbins, McGregor talks about being passionate and the need to be 'all in'. Robbins paraphrasing with, "If you want to take the island you have to burn your boats." If there is a way back, then your head will partially keep you there and your chances of success reduce. But the most important statement in the Robbins interview, in my opinion, is something we all need to remember when we have a period of lull, have a lack of commitment or focus: "your lack of commitment is an insult to the people who believe in you, who love you." If you are not going to make the most of your life for yourself, then you must make the change for those who believe you can.

So, as I continue to say throughout this book, if you don't like your circumstance, your current world, your life as it is, you have the capability to change it, if you want to. You have the capability to transform.

~ 3 ~

As we have just learned even the great Connor McGregor admits to having periods of distraction, lack of commitment and reduced motivation. The reality is that we all have periods of lull. Have you ever asked yourself why intelligent people procrastinate? Why some people, no matter how many opportunities they are presented with just can't seem to get a break in life. Maybe that is you?

Well, I can tell you it is not through a lack of resources. There has never been another time in history when we have had more resources available to us. In the information age in which we live, there is very little you cannot find out through the tap of a keyboard or the swipe of a finger. Money is easy to get. Interest rates are low. Networks are easy to access. Find a group online and infiltrate it.

Resources are not the reason some people find it hard in life. There are plenty of people, well-known people like Einstein, Oprah, Abraham Lincoln and Colonel Sanders who were born into or ended up with nothing and yet still managed to do amazing things. If you want to use a lack of resources and opportunity as an excuse for why things have not really worked out for you, maybe go read up on some of these people.

The reality is that our nervous system is hardwired for comfort whilst our essence, what makes us who we are, wants to grow. We must manage the tension between the two paradigms. It is your ability to overcome that ever-present lean toward procrastination. Sitting on the couch versus going for a run. We need to understand this tension to recognise its presence and stop it from stopping us focusing on our growth, our goals.

To understand this, we need to look at the human brain. Or part of it at least. Specifically, the neo-cortex or frontal lobe. This area of the brain operates at alpha or beta brain waves, but only after age seven. Before age seven the frontal lobe operates at delta of theda wave lengths with no critical thinking. After age seven our critical thinking capability starts to come in. Until we start to be able to critically analyse the information we receive, we pretty much believe everything we are told. This is why children are so impressionable.

Take as an example the last time you did the grocery shopping with the kids. You get to the check out and as every good retailer does, they place the items they want to sell at the eye height of the people they want to sell to. So, your youngest sees the chocolate and asks if they can have one. Now what they don't know is that you have your own shit that you are dealing with – your job that might be on the line, financial concerns (you can't really afford extras now) and the fight you had with your partner that morning. You deny them the desired chocolate. They keep begging and eventually you snap, telling them, "You can't have the chocolate, you don't deserve the chocolate, you haven't been good enough."

Now your child, operating in theda length brain waves, is oblivious to your big world problems and does not hear your frustration, instead they hear, *'I am not worth it, I am not good enough and I am undeserving.'* The chances are your child probably spends a large part of the rest of their life acting out this behaviour to justify why they are right. Including self-sabotage if success threatens to contradict that schema. Remember the schemas we talked about earlier and why sometimes these schemas need adjustment for you to realise that who you think you are, may not necessarily be you?

You can see how an impression made on you subconsciously can sit with you and prevent you from moving forward. Even more so if this early impression is reinforced throughout your life.

Peter Sage is a well-known international serial entrepreneur, author, philosopher, personal growth expert, and teacher. His knowledge in psychology is phenomenal. In fact, a lot of what I have just been speaking about is gleaned from Sage's work. Speaking to this, Sage has found that the first law of psychology is 'people will never rise above the opinion of themselves'. And when this opinion is ingrained in early life and then consolidated by life experience, it is difficult to change.

Add your environment and depending on the positive or negative stimulus you receive from your daily surroundings, the difficulty you have to make change or transform may be pre-determined.

~ 4 ~

Bill Hanagan was a logistic manager with a trucking firm. He had spent years working his way up from the bottom. He was well respected in the business and by his team. Hanagan was happy with life. In his spare time, he was a handy man. There was little he could not fix or build, and his quality of work was high.

In 2018 one of Hanagan's staff made a grave mistake whilst driving the folk lift. The forklift rolled trapping the staff member under the machine and crushing his arm. The incident fractured the humerus (bone in the upper arm) which came through the skin and lacerated the medial artery. It was quite a gruesome scene with significant blood and high levels of chaos as varying people tried to console the driver and deal to the injuries to stop the bleeding and ultimately save the driver's life. Unfortunately, the arm could not be saved, and the driver had the limb amputated a week later.

If the incident was not enough for Hanagan, having seen what he described as a war scene, the aftermath of the incident from the company's perspective was a textbook attempt to divert blame from the company and use Hanagan as a scapegoat.

Standard practice in a serious injury workplace incident means Worksafe are required to undertake an investigation. During the interviews with the staff and in particular the senior managers, the managers blamed Hanagan for failure to operate a safe workplace and failing to lead his staff with an appropriate safety culture. Various parties threatened to sue both the business and Hanagan as an individual. The pressure became too much for Hanagan and his mental health began to suffer.

As is often the case when these types of incidents occur and the individual's involved health is affected, other areas of their life become affected also. Hanagan took some of his frustration out on his family and eventually the toll became too much for his wife who sought companionship elsewhere. She had an affair. The marriage ended.

Hanagan soon met a new partner and they moved in together. Despite the affair, Hanagan remained in contact with his ex-wife who has since married the person she had the affair with. Nevertheless, Hanagan continued to experience symptoms of Post-Traumatic Stress Disorder (PTSD), which again took a toll on his relationship. It should be noted that Hanagan was receiving treatment from a psychologist, psychiatrist and general practitioner. He was also prescribed a heavy dose of anti-depressants. His treating practitioners prognosed that he could not return to his pre-injury employer and Hanagan was medically retired. Forced to find a new career.

It was around this time that I was engaged by his insurance company to help Hanagan transform and realise his new life. Upon recognising that he could not return to his pre-condition employer he decided that he could put his skills as a handy man to work. He would start his own business. Not only would starting a business and being his own manager allow him the flexibility to manage his symptoms around his responsibilities, but it would allow him time to heal, and he could gradually increase his working hours as required.

Over the next few months, I worked with Hanagan to set up his business, develop and implement a marketing strategy, establish a network of customers and referral sources and grow a pipeline of work. Hanagan was all in on his new business and for a while, was distracted from the trauma of his experience. I could see however, that whilst the business was growing fast, Hanagan was not addressing the underlying pathology of his PTSD. He had not 'owned' his part in the incident, and to top it all off his home life with his new partner had become toxic. Hanagan was forced out of his home. He lived in his car for a few nights. Couch surfed with friends before being offered a bed for as long as he needed at his ex-wife's house, complete with the new husband that had been the precipitator to the end of Hanagan's marriage. Hanagan had created the perfect environment for exacerbation of his PTSD symptoms. He lost focus of his business and again his life began to spiral out of control.

It didn't take long before Hanagan fell over. He was unable to function. Debilitated by flashbacks of both the incident and the events that followed. He was catatonic for several weeks and if not for the great collaborative work of his psych team and I to help him realise the toxic mess he had created, an environment that allowed him to be reminded on an hourly basis the pain he had gone through in the last two years both at work and personally, he would have surely reached a point of self-harm.

Thankfully, Hanagan did not reach that point. In fact, we finally got him to realise that he needed to change his environment for him to focus on what was important – creating purpose and a level of self-respect that could carry him through to a positive future, and allow him to transform his life to something that he could enjoy. Once he had this realisation, we were able to redirect him to what needed to be done for his ultimate transformation. As soon as he changed his environment to move away from the constant reinforcement of the past, he was able to move forward.

Hanagan is now happy, healthy, running a successful business and has put his past behind him. He is focused on growing his business and has nothing but positivity for the future. Hanagan is the ultimate example of how your environment can prevent you from being able to focus on what is important.

~ 5 ~

So how do we change our environment and improve our ability to focus? Well, Sage would say you need to do three things:
1)	Stop putting the wrong things in.

2) Start putting the right things in; and
3) Get the things that shouldn't be in there, out!

What does that mean? Unfortunately, in Australia, very few people want to see you succeed. They want to keep you at their level. They don't want you to have aspirations, to reach for the stars or to try and better yourself. They will tell you that it can't be done. They will tell you that what has happened to you is someone else's fault and that you should focus your energy on getting compensation for that perceived wrongdoing. David's story in early chapters ring any bells? But you and I know better! We know after reading the Ownership chapter of this book that whilst others might have contributed to the outcome, ultimately you put yourself in that circumstance. In that environment.

You will likely turn on the TV and be told by the news, that now is not the time to try. The economy is now set to dive. The housing market will plumet and businesses are failing left, right and centre. Your social feeds will serve you up a never-ending stream of minutia designed to remind you of what you haven't got, what others are doing that you will never be able to do; that because of your negative environment, what you would like, you will never have. These very same feeds are designed to distract you from your true destiny, your happiness, and your goals.

Chris Bailey is the international bestselling author of *Hyperfocus* and *The Productivity Project*, which have been published in sixteen languages. Chris works with organisations around the globe on how they can become more productive. He is described by TED as *'the most productive man you'd ever meet'*. Bailey has studied what it takes to be more focused.

According to Bailey's research, with so much technology distracting us, we focus on one task for a maximum of 40 seconds before switching to something else. But what Bailey found out next was mind blowing. It turns out that the reason our level of focus is so low is not because we are distracted by technology, it is because our brains are over stimulated. We crave stimulation.

You, as the reader of this book, know it. How many times have you looked at your phone whilst reading this book? Or even just noted the familiar *'ding'* of a notification that you now can't stop thinking about and desperately want to see? And when you do, your brain rewards you with a hit of dopamine – that brain chemical that makes you feel good.

So, Bailey continued his research. He wanted to find out what would happen if our over-stimulated brain was less stimulated. He conducted an experiment where for one hour per day he did nothing. He did this for 30 days straight. What he found is that after eight days, his desire to seek stimulation reduced and his desire continued to reduce as the days increased throughout the experiment. More importantly, Bailey discovered his ability to focus improved. His ability to produce more and new ideas increased and he was able to plan his time better. Why? Because his brain was allowed to wander more without distraction.

If you think about this, it makes sense. I know that when I am contemplating a problem, I am often paralysed by what to do until I change my environment and withdraw (only for a few minutes) from all the other distractions in my life. My ideas on how to solve the problem or find a pathway to achieve the goal I have been chasing often come to me in the shower, or when I take a walk around the block. Or when I'm in that zone of not being asleep (but not quite awake either) at night when you go to bed. My favourite space. I wish I could live there.

Keith Richards, the lead guitarist for the Rolling Stones once claimed that it was in this space that the rift for the song 'Satisfaction' came to him. He awoke and, in that space of slight disorientation, he was hit with it. If you are too young to know the song I am talking about, download it. It is catchy. After that, Richards apparently started sleeping with his guitar and is rumoured to have slept in a chair holding a handful of bolts over a steel plate. When he went to sleep the bolts would drop out of his hand onto the plate and wake him. All so he could have time in what I have termed the 'slake' (sleep/wake) zone.

Back to Bailey. According to Bailey's research, it turns out that when we let our brains be less stimulated and able to wander, we think about three main things: the past (12% of the time), the present (28% of the time) and the future (48% of the time). This is called the mind prospectus bias and clearly shows that by creating more space in our minds we can better focus. In fact, Bailey believes that it is not distraction that is the enemy of focus, it is *overstimulation* that is the enemy of focus. Thus, stop letting people and technology fill your mind with the wrong things, the negative things, the things that will reduce your confidence. Surround yourself with positive stimulus or to improve your focus, no stimulus at all. Not completely. Just for short periods of time like Bailey.

What about 'putting the right things in'? Well, that is a matter of surrounding yourself with the right people and the right feeds of information that encourage you, that fill your bucket and give you the strength to move forward, grow, and believe. A network of stimulus that supports your direction. Having a positive network comes back to Sage's espousals on environment and is something we will talk about in the chapters to come. For now, all you need to know is that if your network believes in you, you have a better chance of believing in yourself. When you believe in yourself, you tend to focus better.

When it comes to getting the things that shouldn't be in there, out, this is where you have to do the work. You must master you! What excites you? Why do you behave in certain ways? What drives you? What distracts you? How do you operate best? What makes you feel the ways you feel when certain things happen? By knowing these things, you can master self, and by mastering self, you can be the creator of your life. You can change this life you desire to change. You can become the new and transformed you.

This is a journey that only you can make. One that starts by answering the above questions and continue by diving deeper into each to uncover the true essence of yourself. By doing this work your life will be vastly improved. Transform even.

But Adam, this doesn't help me now, you say. How can I focus better *now?* That is easy! Start practising. I needed to take you through this chapter's journey on overstimulation so that you understand you are overstimulated and that it is this overstimulation that is causing you to lack focus. I also needed you to understand that by eliminating stimulation, you can greatly improve your focus.

So, here are some of my tips to help you become more focused now.

1. Get Rid Of Distractions

We have already talked about this, so not much more needs to be said. Simply give yourself more time for your brain to wander, and in between those times, start with the simple things like:
- moving to a quiet area
- turning off notifications on your phone or turning your phone off altogether
- closing the door to your office
- telling those around you not to distract you for a period
- closing out of programs or apps that aren't essential on your computer

2. Coffee In Small Doses

According to several studies, drinking coffee or other caffeinated beverages in small doses may have a positive impact on your ability to focus

The key to taking advantage of caffeine's focus-enhancing properties is to consume it in moderation. If you drink too much of it, you may end up feeling anxious or nervous, which generally reduces your ability to stay focused. Trust me, I know on this one – I stopped drinking coffee three years ago for this exact reason. My stable mood and objectivity (which I love having back) is the reward for the loss of something I really enjoyed. The savouring of that first coffee in the morning, ahh!

3. Practise The Pomodoro Technique

Staying focused helps you get more done in less time. While that sounds simple enough, it's not always easy to put into practise. So, the next time you're wrestling with your attention span, try the Pomodoro technique.

This timing method helps you train your brain to stay on task for short periods of time. Here's how it works:
- set your timer for 25 minutes and get to work
- when the buzzer sounds, take a 5-minute break
- then, set the timer again and get back to work

Once you've done four rounds of this, you can take a longer break, approximately 20 to 30 minutes.

4. Put A Lock On Social Media

Most phones and/or apps have the ability to block notifications or silence them for a period. Look into this as it adds to what we have been talking about in this chapter.

5. Fuel Your Body

We all know what happens when "h-anger" strikes. This dreaded combination of hunger and anger is a major focus fail.

So, to keep your brain focused, your energy levels up, and your emotions on an even keel, make sure you don't delay or skip meals. Try to balance lean protein, complex carbohydrates, and healthy fats to stay fuelled. Snack on fresh fruit, veggies, nuts, or seeds if you get hungry between meals, and be sure to keep yourself hydrated with plenty of water.

And, for an extra boost, Harvard Medical School says to include a few of these 'best brain foods' in your day:
- green, leafy vegetables like kale, spinach, and broccoli
- fatty fish such as salmon
- berries, like blueberries, strawberries, raspberries, or blackberries
- walnuts
- tea and coffee for the caffeine, in moderation as discussed

TRANSFORM YOUR LIFE

I eat five small meals per day, but I am also at the gym every day.

6. Get Enough Sleep

It's no secret that the majority of Australians are lacking in sleep. While a few nights of minimal sleep is okay, not getting enough sleep most nights of the week can negatively impact both your short and long-term memory, as well as your ability to concentrate.

The recommended amount of sleep for adults aged 18 to 60 years old is seven or more hours a night. Older adults may need up to 9 hours per night.

To boost your sleep health, try to:
- avoid caffeinated beverages after lunchtime
- switch off all electronic devices an hour before bedtime. The light from these devices can stimulate your brain and prevent you from feeling sleepy
- take time to wind down. Read a book, take a warm bath, listen to mediative music (I recommend Insight Timer – its free and chocka block full of something you will like)
- keep your bedroom cool and quiet. According to the Cleveland Clinic, an ideal temperature is between 60 and 67°F (15.6 and 19.4°C) – the lower end of this temperature range more recommended
-

7. Set A SMART Goal

If your lack of focus is a result of feeling overwhelmed by a complex project, try breaking it down into smaller parts and plugging the smaller steps into the SMART formula.

SMART stands for:

Specific: What exactly needs to be done?
Measurable: How will you track your progress?
Achievable: Is it realistic? Can it be done by the deadline?
Relevant: How does it fit with the plan or bigger goal?

Timely: When does it need to be done?

When you take a large, complex project and break it down into smaller, bite-size tasks you can boost your ability to concentrate and focus on specific tasks. That's because you end up with goals you actually feel like you can accomplish.

Matthew Michalewicz, entrepreneur and author of *Life in Half a Second*, one of my favourite books proposes the pyramid model which I use to create smart goals and to break my overall goals into smaller pieces.

Basic Model

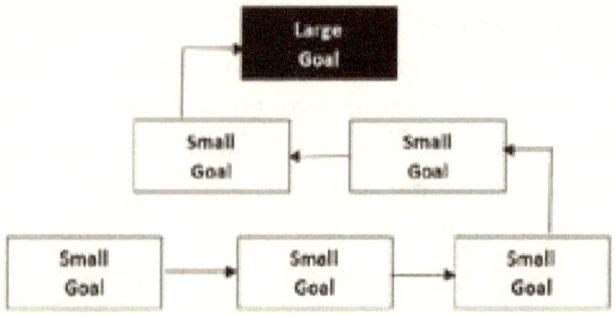

The basic premise of the model is to break your large goals into small goals that work toward your large goal. You can add in accountability by adding timeframes.

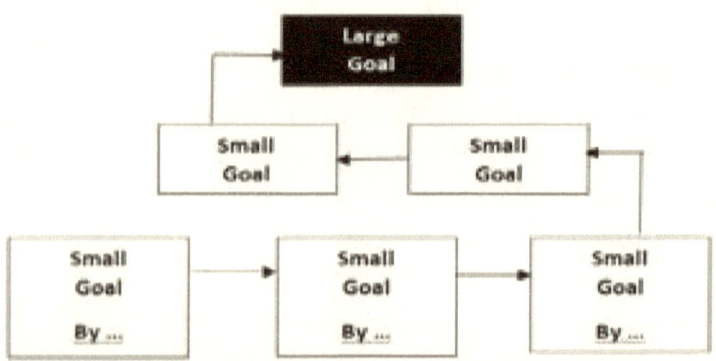

Back in Chapter Two you drafted your long-lost goals; now transfer these goals into your pyramid. Remember, they are only your top square. Once you have the goal in the top square you need to break the goal down into smaller steps that work toward your large goal. Your pyramid may have two or three small steps, or it may have 20 or more. Whatever you need to work toward it.

In an early chapter we talked about the rate of people feeling successful being 8%. The other 92% set their goals and don't put in enough steps to make their goal achievable. The smaller you make the small steps and easier to achieve, the more likely you are to accomplish each and the more likely it will be that you feel successful.

And don't forget to reward yourself when you achieve each step, and then a big reward when you reach your large goal.

Last, put a note in your diary to review the pyramid weekly and adjust if things happen that prevent you from meeting your small target. Things will happen and often those things might be out of your control. Don't sweat it! Just make the adjustment and focus on the next key date. It is not about the destination. Often the journey is the fun part.

8. Be More Mindful

According to the Mayo Clinic, being mindful means you can maintain moment-to-moment awareness of where you are and what you're doing, which is great news when you're trying to stay focused.

By being mindful and recognising when your attention starts to drift, you can quickly bring your focus back to where it needs to be. Plus, you can train your brain to be more mindful by practising breathing techniques, meditation, and mindful movement, such as yoga.

9. Make A To-Do List

Let's face it. The items on a to-do list can add up quickly. And it can be challenging to find the motivation to accomplish everything you set out to do.

The good news? Studies show that having a written plan of action can increase productivity.

After you make your list, choose two or three key tasks and put them at the top. Then rank the rest of the items in order of importance. This allows you to tackle urgent tasks when your brain is fresh, and your energy levels are high.

Consider your goal to be achievement of the top three items for the day. If you achieve them, you can start some of the other tasks. If you don't, then they become the priority for tomorrow. What you will find is that some of the tasks on the list will start to fall off the bottom. They were not the priority you thought they were, and this again allows you to add new priorities or spend more time achieving the ones of more significance.

With each task, don't forget to ask yourself: 'Will doing this task help me to reach my goal'? If the answer is no, then cross it off and go to a task that will.

10. Do Similar Tasks

Tired of jumping from one type of thinking to another (aka 'multitasking')? Then pick tasks that are similar, group them together, and do one at a time. This makes transitions smoother, and you may find that you get a lot more done by not jumping from one type of task to another.

Despite what you may think, multitasking is not more effective or efficient, especially when you're struggling with staying focused. In fact, the American Psychological Association reports that multitasking may reduce productivity by as much as 40 percent.

The bottom line: whether you're dealing with too many competing priorities, lack of sleep, or just a simple dose of the

'Mondays', not being able to focus can really put a damper on your productivity.

That's why it's important to have a few simple tips and tricks, like the ones we described above, at your fingertips. Knowing how to zone in on what needs to get done can help you stay on track with your most important tasks each day.

As Winston Churchill said, 'You will never reach your destination if you stop and throw stones at every dog that barks'. So, focus on the things that are going to help you achieve your goal.

The final thing to remember is that like that espoused in the Ownership chapter, you are responsible for your focus. Only you can help yourself to focus and achieve your goal. To truly transform your life, you must be self-reliant.

Chapter 6

SELF-RELIANCE

You never know how strong you are until being strong is your only choice.

– Bob Marley

~ 1 ~

Jessica Watson (OAM) navigated some of the world's most remote oceans and survived seven knockdowns and 210 days alone at sea to become the youngest person to sail solo, nonstop around the world, aged 16. On completion of the voyage, Jessica was met by the then Prime Minister who declared her an Australian hero. In a simple speech that won admiration across Australia and around the world, she responded to the Prime Minister by announcing that she disagreed with him, that she didn't consider herself a hero—just an 'ordinary person, who had a dream, worked hard at it and proved that anything really is possible'.

~ 2 ~

It takes a remarkable feat of self-reliance for anyone to battle the world's oceans solo for 210 days, let alone a 16-year-old. But as Watson said, she is an ordinary person, who had a dream, worked hard at it and proved that anything really is possible. Whilst this is true, Watson also proved that self-reliance is not just about being independent and is not about being individualistic. Watson had a huge support team to make her dream come true. So, it is not about doing it all yourself, being self-reliant is everything we have talked about in this book – ownership, intuition, moving with change and focus. It is about showing people that you have charge of your life, so they are willing to help you move forward faster.

Ralph Waldo Emerson may not have introduced the concept, but it was he who brought it to the public with his 1841 essay: Self-Reliance. Whilst it was he who first brought it to the world's cognition, there is no single sentence—not even from Emerson himself—that really captures all the aspects of self-reliance. Merriam Webster tries to define self-reliance, as: 'reliance on one's own efforts and abilities' which, when looking at the great feats achieved by people like Watson and others, does not capture the use of networks and supports to really tap into your own efforts and abilities.

In an age where statistics allows almost everything to be psychometrically measured, and operational definitions proliferate, it isn't surprising there's no one definition for self-reliance. Linked to identity with 'the self'—in its psychological sense (Baumeister, 1987) it has been alluded to roughly in psychological journals as: 'a reliance on internal resources to provide life with coherence (meaning) and fulfillment' (Baumeister, 1987: 171). Again, far from an encapsulation of what it really takes to be self-reliant.

Self-Reliance is the topic (and title) of the 1841 essay from US philosopher Ralph Waldo Emerson. Born in Boston in 1803, Emerson wrote poetry and gave lectures that would greatly influence other famous names such as Henry Thoreau and Walt Whitman (IEP, 2019).

Self-Reliance (the poem) contains Emerson's beliefs and perspectives on how society negatively impacts our growth. He argues strongly that self-reliance, self-trust, and individualism, amongst other things, are ways that we can avoid the conformity imposed upon us. Or, that we quite frequently impose upon ourselves.

He examples some key concepts of self-reliance as:

1. Thinking Independently

The ability to think autonomously goes hand in hand with trusting your own instinct as we discussed in the chapter entitled 'Intuition'. Lots of Emerson's work centred on how people tend to 'hide behind' what they've learned from society or learned from significant others within society and not go after their true calling. He believed this was mere imitation and was linked with a lack of confidence in one's own intuition and rational capabilities. Sound familiar?

Basically, if you (or I, or anyone) believe in something and consider that it holds merit after thinking it through, there should be nothing holding us back from moving forward with confidence. Not to do so, Emerson believed, is to conform to societal expectations (like sheep) for no good reason.

2. Embracing Your Individuality

As a more practical example, we can imagine that Frank has parents who are both doctors. They want nothing more than for Frank to follow in their footsteps and are reassured by his excellent grades at school.

At home, however, Frank finds that he spends every spare minute playing guitar. He wants to make a difference to the world and touch people's lives through music. This is where he finds his greatest happiness and decides instead to pursue a career as a musician.

3. Striving Toward Your Own Goals, Bravely

In an extension of the above, Frank seeks to take steps toward achieving his own goals of becoming a lead guitarist in a rock band. He's aware that he'll receive a lot more emotional and financial support by following his parents' desires, but he's willing to take a chance. Because Frank believes that purposeful action will help him achieve his goals, he isn't concerned about rejection by his parents because he wants to be his own man.

These are just three examples based on Emerson's original paper on self-reliance and represent the three concepts most closely related to individualism: thinking independently, embracing your individuality, and striving toward your own goals. It's important to remember here, though, that self-reliance is not about cutting yourself off from everybody. In fact, using your network and support structures (as exampled by Jessica Watson) to make your desires reality is a key part of being self-reliant. More shortly.

This is more about being true to yourself, being capable of independent thought, knowing your own loves and needs and being able to pursue them independently of others' judgements. It's not the same as isolating yourself from society.

Whilst Emerson does expand considerably on the value of solitude, the idea of social networks—of having friends—features strongly in his work. We'll touch on these shortly when we look at how to develop self-reliance.

So why is it so important to be self-reliant?

It's important for several reasons. The most obvious being that depending on others for help means there will be times when it's not available. At these times you need to be able to solve problems and make decisions by yourself. This is critical in transforming your life after incident or injury, and in helping you to feel happy by yourself, in yourself, and about yourself – taking control of your life without needing to rely on others.

But something you must consider is that by having self-reliance and driving your goals forward independently, people will want to help. People love to see go-getters chase their passion and will nearly always want to be part of something positive. Especially helping someone to move forward after adversity.

As we discussed in the chapter on 'Ownership' and 'Change', self-acceptance is a very powerful thing to have, and acquiring self-knowledge and practising self-compassion and allowing yourself to move forward and transform your life after an incident, you gain a new perspective, which in turn…

Gives you direction.

~ 3 ~

Jonathan Yulison was a former police officer who had dabbled in property investment on the side. In 2018 after witnessing some horrific events in the course of his employment he began to experience symptoms of Post-Traumatic Stress Disorder (PTSD). His ability to function as a police officer diminished and he was forced to purge from the force. He accessed his income protection, and I was brought in as a business coach to help him set up a business in property.

Yulison had originally conceived the idea after watching property advocates represent buyers. In the traditional model the buyer pays the advocate to find and purchase a property on their behalf. Yulison saw an opportunity to reverse this model, advocate for the buyer but be paid by the vendor. He would source property developers for new developments and create a pool of properties he could sell to property investors. He would then set about creating enquiry from investors that did not have the time or the desire to search for an investment.

I met with Yulison in early 2021 and we quickly developed a great rapport. We worked through his goals for the business, and he informed me of his desire to engage staff to grow the business quickly, that he had already sold two properties and had a further three potential investors looking to meet with him to start the process of him finding an investment property. What he needed help with was marketing and managing his mental health around the demands of starting and running your own business.

Considering Yulison's needs, we developed a marketing strategy which involved engaging staff to develop business, mining of a database of new clients, and managing a portfolio of customers. Consulting and advocacy businesses usually gain clients from word of mouth. Previous customers refer in, and so it is a matter of leveraging your network to get a business in this sector operational.

Yulison turned out to be an expert in this and almost completely self-reliant. I usually run my sessions monthly; meeting with the client for one to two hours a month and we set some agreed action items. In Yulison's case he used me as a sounding board, someone to hold him accountable and someone with experience having set up businesses, grown businesses and sold businesses, to develop a business plan. We would set the action items and he would take them to the next level.

After just three business mentoring sessions Yulison had networked some contacts to identify and on-board a business partner with a complementary set of skills to his own. He had persuaded the partner to buy into the business, thereby improving his own financial position by banking the capital investment of the partner. He had increased his sales by a further three (total now five) and was well on target to his goal of 10 sales for the first financial year.

Even more impressive was that Yulison had conceived, developed and written a 28-day program. A marketing funnel called 'Healthy, Wealthy and Wise', which provided customers with:

Healthy: a one-on-one session with a personal trainer and a one-on-one session with a nutritionist. The aim being to help people improve their health in the program's overall goal of creating a better life for the participant.

Wealthy: a one-on-one session with a financial advisor and a one-on-one session with Yulison. The purpose being for people to understand how they could improve their financial position and work toward their future financial goals. One of which was owning an investment property found and purchased on your behalf by Yulison. The participants in the program would be carefully vetted to ensure they had the means to invest in property.

Wise: a one-on-one session with a mindset coach. This session's aim was to create a more positive approach to life.

The whole program was only $295. When working properly, the program would create a pipeline of investors using Yulison to buy property on their behalf.

I love this idea, but what I love more is that Yulison had the drive and the fortitude to use his own innate knowledge and capability to develop the program whilst leveraging his network – contacts in personal training, nutrition, finance, and wellbeing – to make his dream a reality. That is the true definition of self-reliance.

Of course, Yulison now no longer needs me, and his business has gone from strength to strength and taken him to earning a growing six-figure salary annually. Not only that but the business allows him to manage his family commitments, always being available for the children and his wife, and manage his health. His PTSD is all but dissipated, and what symptoms do arise, Yulison now knows how to manage. Overall, Yulison has been able to transform his life from one of misery, of being consumed by PTSD and ill health to thriving and an endless sunlit horizon.

Now can you see how self-reliance is not just about being independent and going it alone. It is seeing and employing the resources around you.

So how do you develop self-reliance?

~ 4 ~

In an article on developing self-reliance, mental health counsellor Mandy Kloppers offers several practical steps.

1. Accepting Yourself And Being Your Own Best Friend
Learning and appreciating your own character strengths is very important in being able to support yourself as you go through life. What are your character strengths? Are you kind? Curious? Brave? Don't forget to reflect on your achievements and the things you accomplish that make you feel proud. It's important not to put yourself down or sabotage your own efforts.

2. Inner Confidence
In society, we're conditioned to feel happy when we receive compliments, praise, and reassurance from others. If that's not forthcoming, we can feel insecure or vulnerable, sometimes even helpless. Being self-reliant involves the ability to feel confident in yourself when these aren't around, because they may not always be. Not sure what to be confident about? Try one of the activities at the end of the chapter to increase your sense of self-worth.

3. Making Our Own Decisions
Kloppers advises against looking consistently outside for security and relying on others to accept us for who we are. That means you can get rid of your social media! Well, maybe not all of it, but don't take it so literally. When we can accept ourselves as unique and practise non-judgement, we can find security from inner sources. Remember Bailey's social media reduction strategy here.

This rational, independent thinking is something we've already touched on. As children, we learn to look to others for guidance when solving problems or making decisions. The tendency becomes ingrained within us, and as adults, we aren't always capable of handling adversity in a way that we feel sure about. Have confidence in your own capabilities and it becomes a lot easier to find security within and find people that are willing to help you move forward.

4. Recognise And Manage Dependence

Becoming aware of when you tend to turn to others is a part of self-knowledge. We may know that we turn to others for certain things but sometimes this means we're missing out on a chance to build up our own confidence. Setting goals and achieving them your own way not only gives you a sense of accomplishment and reward but greater belief in your own judgement.

When I was CEO of the NSCA I used to hate it when my staff would come to me with problems and no solutions. They were looking to me to solve the problem for them. So I spent some time working with them to understand that they needed to evaluate the issue and the potential solutions to allow the management team to work each solution through and initiate the best solution for the business. It was only through everyone's independent work being presented to the rest of the management team that allowed the management team to help that person solve the problem as a group. Without their individual work, the management team were not willing to help.

5. Accept Yourself For Who You Are

Self-acceptance is a huge thing. Instead of looking to others for approval, it's all right to give that approval yourself. We discussed this in the chapter on 'Ownership'. Seeking others' acceptance is yet another way that we practise dependence on others, and it can be a pervasive, hard-to-shake habit. To develop self-reliance, we need to notice these tendencies before we can change them and sometimes this can't be done on our own, we need help. (See Chapter 1.)

Would you believe it? Here are even more ways to develop self-reliance:

1. Having Your Own Values

Society's values may not be aligned with our own deep-rooted beliefs. This can be at such a subconscious level that we don't always pick up on it. If society values one thing, and it's not congruent with our own, we can feel as though it's hard to gain acceptance.

For example, you may value diversity and inclusiveness but maybe work somewhere that doesn't. This creates cognitive dissonance that can be unpleasant to deal with (Fostinger, 1957). We must separate from this environment (as discussed in the chapter on 'Focus'), and start putting the right stuff in.

2. Not Relying On 'Things' To Feel Happiness

Emerson argued strongly about the potential negative influences of material possessions; he was of the belief that we live in materialistic times. Life is constantly changing; if we tie our happiness to external objects, what happens when they're gone?

My mate Tony Robbins (I've never met him, so he is only my mate in my head) talks about his humble beginnings and how the universe will provide. He believes you will receive ten-times what positive energy you put out into the universe. Once, when he had only $10 to his name, he saw a homeless man who clearly needed the money more than Robbins. He gave the man the $10 and went to find a place to sleep for the night. Two days later Robbins chanced upon a man who afforded him the opportunity to sell an item for a $100 commission. Robbins sold the item and earned the money. This opportunity later led him to his role on infomercials selling products on TV, allowing him to transform his life to the Tony Robbins we now know and love.

For interest's sake, Tony Robbins infomercials are still played every 90 seconds somewhere in the world.

3. Decide Who You Want To Be, And How You Want To Get There

Pretty much, this is almost the same as having your own values. Except that once we know our own values, we can understand what makes us happy and how we would like to live our lives. Then, we exercise our own judgement about how we want to get there (as discussed in the 'Intuition' chapter).

Basically, this discussion has covered exactly what this book is about. Recognise who you are, decide what you want to do, make the change, focus on your goal, and leverage your abilities and the resources around you. Emphasise the utilisation of resources around you and make sure you don't go excessive on your individualism.

~ 5 ~

As discussed throughout this chapter, an excess of individualism can obviously lead one to become an isolated loner or act with great selfishness. Done right, however, individualism has tremendous benefits for our sense of competence, effectiveness, and life direction. Our overall wellbeing and mental health.

Scholars have described individualism in three dimensions: a belief in one's responsibility for one's actions; a belief in one's uniqueness; and a tendency to set and strive for one's personal goals. All competencies that, when held, provide us a true sense of mastery and control and therefore a true sense of wellbeing.

Just as some people are more individualistic than others, countries vary in the level of individualism in their cultures. In one multination study using a measure commonly cited in academic research, the United States and the United Kingdom were found to have the most individualistic cultures, followed by Australia, the Netherlands, and Canada. The least individualistic countries assessed were Venezuela, Colombia, Pakistan, and Indonesia.

As a general rule, researchers find that individualism in a country strongly predicts the average level of wellbeing even when correcting for life expectancy, access to food and water, and other variables. Scholars offer two main explanations. The first is that in individualistic cultures, people spend time and effort pursuing personal happiness over honour and social obligations. This view assumes that working for happiness ultimately leads to greater wellbeing, which the research supports. Some researchers have even argued that positive psychology, which is based on the belief that your happiness is important, worthy of study, and at least partly under your control, is at the core of an individualistic worldview.

The second explanation is that individualism is associated with 'open societies', which have a high degree of freedom of expression and self-actualisation. This, in turn, fosters tolerance, trust, and civic engagement while minimising outside pressure on how one must live. In an open society, people make the most of their own decisions about their profession, education, marital status, geography, religion, etc., ideally in a way that is consistent with their wellbeing.

Something that needs to be considered in all this is that these happiness benefits require individualists live in individualistic societies; in more collectivist cultures, a different pattern tends to emerge. Research has shown, for example, that in the relatively collectivistic Japan and Portugal, students and workers who have individualistic values tend to suffer lower wellbeing than the national average. Individualists are misfits in a collectivist setting and, as the research shows, struggle to find camaraderie, which is central to happiness.

They might even be tempted to leave, which could help explain the worldly growth in migration to predominant individualistic countries like the United States, a nation built by immigrants. Research has shown that immigrants to the United States have a greater sense of self-reliance and personal agency than non-immigrants. One way to stop being a misfit, it seems, is to join a country of misfits.

No matter your personal and cultural orientations, you can improve your wellbeing with some good individualistic practises. "Whoso would be a man must be a nonconformist," Emerson wrote in Self-Reliance. Substitute 'a man' for 'happy' and we might have some indication of what Emerson is implying.

It is difficult when we read this not to want to go it alone, but we must remember what self-reliance means. It does not mean isolation. Think of the individualists suffering in collectivist settings not because they think for themselves but because they tend to become isolated and friendless. There is no evidence that individualists suffer less from loneliness or are less social than collectivists. Almost no one thrives in isolation as we have seen from our collective experience of COVID lockdown and 14-day isolations.

But that doesn't mean you have to suppress your individuality to make friends with people who simply don't get you. For example, does your workplace demand a suffocating degree of conformism? Are you uncomfortable in the way you are expected to dress, talk, and act? It might be a good idea to look at the job market or, as I am suggesting, transform your life to one that really fits your sense of purpose.

Similarly, if you are a student, does your school value and protect a diversity of viewpoints? Or is only one way of thinking acceptable? If the latter, you might want to study elsewhere, at a place that values independent thought.

Second, do think for yourself. In a world that is moved by ideas, there is arguably no greater force for progress than intellectual nonconformism. We have no other way to solve previously unsolvable problems, and it is people like you that think outside the box and with a willingness to give it a go that will solve these problems. In doing so, creating a better world.

As I write this book, big topics are climate change, equality, women's rights and where men sit in society as women start to do what was previously only the 'territory' for men. These issues all come with a high need for nonconformists to think beyond that of previous generations to bring these topics into balance and solve the most challenging of current concerns.

It is not just us being allowed to think for ourselves though. This requires allowing others to think for themselves as well. America's polarised culture has an alarming tendency to proclaim, when it comes to opinions, 'individualism for me, but collectivism for thee'. Part of being a true individualist is fighting for the right of others to not correspond to traditional ideas. Each of us can do this by defying those who would curb free speech in politics, in business, and on campuses. It is especially effective when we stand up to bullies on our own side of the argument.

"Apolitical victory, a rise of rents, the recovery of your sick, or the return of your absent friend, or some other favourable event, raises your spirits, and you think good days are preparing for you," Emerson wrote at the end of his essay. "Do not believe it. Nothing can bring you peace but yourself."

This is something I am always telling my kids. The only person that can make you happy is yourself, and that no matter your circumstance a positive view will go a long way to making positive progress. Once again, we must remember that it is not just us that creates our happiness. We co-create our happiness through faith (if this applies), family, and friendship. But Emerson's main point is indispensable: If you're not in charge of your life through thick and thin, little progress is possible.

My final point here circles back to this chapter's opening point. When you take charge of your life other people will recognise your effort and be willing to help. If you are not helping yourself, few will be willing to help you.

This point is illustrated by recent events in Afghanistan. For the last 20 years the United States and other coalition forces have fought to take back the country from the Taliban and return it to a democracy. After years of fighting, training an Afghan force to safeguard the country and re-instating a stable government, the United States, together with the coalition forces decided it was time to return the country to its people. Within five days of United States and coalition withdrawal, the Taliban had taken back full control of the country. The Afghan forces surrendered without firing a bullet. When challenged by the press that the withdrawal was too soon, Joe Biden, The President of the United States said, "I am no longer willing to place Americans in harm's way for something the Afghanistan people are not willing to fight for themselves."

So go forth, people, start fighting for what you want, work toward your life's goals and other people will be willing to help.

To aid you in your start, and to close-out this chapter here are some activities to help you develop self-reliance.

Activity 1 – I Am And I Can

This one's a group activity. The underpinning theory of this exercise is that you can develop a sense of your own competence by learning to identify your own strengths as a person. These can include unique capabilities, talents, and characteristics. Once you become aware of these, you can tune into these positive aspects in difficult situations.

You will need some large pieces of paper, drawing materials, and some space for the group.

Start by inviting the participants to think of things they can do well, and which make them feel good about that ability. This is tough because we do not often turn the spotlight on ourselves and celebrate our capabilities, so you might like to push this even further to then play a round of 'I am good at…', in which you take turns to chat about these things by finishing the sentence. If you find that one or more are having difficulty identifying a skill or trait and don't feel they can respond, ask another person (especially one who knows that person) to step in with something they believe that person does well.

Then, talk about how learning is a lifelong activity – it's something we never stop doing and we are always learning new skills. You can use this opportunity to go back over the things they've just said, which they didn't have a few years ago. Share one of your own learning experiences and note any difficulties you encountered but end with how satisfying it was to finally learn that skill.

End with a group round of 'I can…', giving the participants a chance to re-affirm their beliefs in their strengths.

Activity 2 – Getting Organised
Another great self-reliance activity is scheduling your own time.

This is a simplified exercise centred on individualism and personal responsibility, two of the main points of this chapter.

It's as simple as asking them to create their own timetable for reaching their weekly, monthly, annual, or long-term goals. You can use the model provided in the 'Focus' chapter. This works especially well for people with anxiety, teaching that getting there in the future means organising now and being organised can reduce their anxiety. They can also get affirmation about their achievements by logging when they accomplish a certain task or goal.

Headings you may find useful for a timetable include:
Goal: what you want to achieve.
Step: the steps required to get there. There may be more than one step to achieve the goal.
Resources: whose help or what will I need to achieve this.
Achievement date.

Make sure you pin this one to the wall to drive and motivate as you smash your goals out of the park.

3. Personal Mission Statement
Personal Mission Statements ask people to think about who they are, what they represent, what they want to accomplish,

and why. They encourage self-reliance by inviting the writer to look inside themselves and seek their own values and beliefs.

This activity becomes more of a framework, and it asks a person to answer three questions so they can craft their own statement:

Outline your perfect day with unlimited resources. Describe as much as you can about your passions and interests.

Imagine you're happily surrounded by your family at the age of 150. What would you tell them about the most important things in life?

Pretend it's a significant milestone at a later stage in life; maybe you've turned 30, 50, or 80. The press asks you to summarise your accomplishments and think about what you'd hope your colleagues, peers, and family to say when discussing you. How would you like to have made a difference in their lives?

The next part is for the writer to review the answers to these questions. The idea is that these should give them valuable help to answer the questions above. That is, as noted above: who they are, what do they represent, what do they want to accomplish, and why.

Chapter 7

TRANSFORM

The cave you fear to enter holds the treasure that you seek.
— Joseph Campbell

~ 1 ~

Once upon time in a forest there was a tiger cub in amongst a flock of sheep. He ate grass and he wandered around with the sheep. When he tried to say anything all that came out was a little meow. Not much of a roar.

One day through the forest came a large male tiger. He's just about to pounce on a sheep and he sees this tiger cub. He says, 'what are you doing here?' The tiger cub replies, 'Baaaaaaa'. The big male tiger picks the cub up by the scruff of the neck and he carries him over to a pond. He puts the cub's face over it and says, 'look, you're not a sheep, you're a tiger.'

The male tiger says, 'ok, we need to do something.' He slays a sheep, and he grabs a big hunk of raw meat and shoves it in the little tiger's mouth. The little tiger gagged on it, as all do on the truth, but it went down. He got a little bit of energy and soon he had a bigger tiger roar. Eventually he had a full tiger roar, and he went off with the male tiger.

(Finding Joe – YouTube, 2020)

So, there you have it. The Five Bridges you need to cross to successfully transform your life after injury, a mental health episode or if you simply don't like the life you live. But what is with the story about the tiger cub, you may be asking. Isn't the moral of the story evident?

If you are a tiger living amongst sheep, you are a poor specimen of a tiger. We are all tigers living amongst sheep. We are all individuals living with a 'self' that we don't even begin to understand. To take it further and to draw from some of what we learned in Chapter 5 and the work of Peter Sage, the food we get from the culture around us (our environment, the people we surround ourselves with) is perhaps food for sheep. It is not food for tigers.

Do you want to be the tiger or the sheep? Do you want to be the hero of your story or wake up on your death bed wishing you made a change when you had the chance?

~ 2 ~

If you look at the classic hero's story—reincarnated in nearly every movie, book, fable or myth—the hero is provided a period of separation where their life is called into question, and they realise they are different, or things need to be different. That is you right now. You have been injured, physically or mentally, or you just don't like the life you are living. You realise something needs to change. You wouldn't have picked up this book otherwise, and you certainly would not have read the book to this point if you aren't looking for more.

The hero is then called to adventure and goes through a period of re-invention, of testing and trials. Where dragons (metaphor of personal troubles) appear. These dragons are only seen by the hero. They are the hero's dragons. The things that stop the hero from fulfilling their destiny, that block the path. To move forward the hero must face these dragons and in doing so acquires a greater strength. Something that is already inside them but is brought to the surface by the trials they face and, as we learned in Chapter 6 as well as with the story of the little tiger, help the hero claim their inner resources.

At the conclusion of these trials, the hero then emerges from the dark into the light. From an unsatisfying life to a satisfying life. The holy grail, if you will. Where the holy grail (not in the sense of the biblical chalice holding the meaning of life), rather the combination of the hero's needs fulfilled to create their ultimate life. The hero then returns to live that life happily ever after.

Sounds familiar, doesn't it? That is because you have seen it a thousand times in books, movies, news articles and some real-life examples such as those provided in this book.

> *Your life is the fruit of your own doing.*
> *You have no one to blame but yourself.*
>
> – Joseph Campbell

But the world doesn't want you to be the hero! Society wants to keep you in your place and has designed it to do so. There is tremendous pressure, even in the media, in keeping people in their place. In the sense of keeping them happy, tranced-out consumers. It's a trance of comfort, of not sticking your head up above the crowd; that keeps the enterprise going. We have been led to believe that staying home and watching TV is a privilege. The bigger the TV, the better. And, we the consumer, space out. We are not developing. We are taught that it is about collecting things and making a lot of money, but it is impossible to enjoy that. Society wants you to stay in place and feeds you subliminal messages day in and day out to keep you on the treadmill. It is a treadmill that very few will get off. Society would like you to stay on that treadmill and not disturb the status quo. That is why people don't like to see you succeed. Australia especially has the 'tall poppy syndrome', where people will ridicule you and attempt to and make you feel bad for trying to do better. That is why few people transform their lives.

As we read in Chapter 2 ('Intuition'), we already know what we want and what to do to fulfill our destiny. Your intuition will remind you. Strangely, when the calling is big enough and you continue to ignore it, the universe will continue to call until you answer. It is that voice in the back of your head telling you that you are not in the right place. That knot in your stomach, anxiously making you feel that you need to be somewhere else. That vision of a future far different from your current reality that you have not gone after. These are the signs that so many people ignore, and by doing so, never transform their lives and become the person they were always meant to be.

These signs are never stronger than when you are in the depth of despair. When you feel at rock bottom. It is at this time when the universe will upend you. As it has now with your injury, ill health and/or unsatisfying life. When this happens, you have three possible paths:

1) Surrender to victimhood.

2) Give your life to someone else and let them tell you what to do; or

3) Take control.

To quote Nietzsche, 'The snake who cannot shed its skin must perish'.

This means to take control you must kill your old life and commit to creating your new one.

We must be willing to get rid of the life we've planned so as to have the life that is waiting for us.

– Joseph Campbell

We must be willing to make change as we discussed in Chapter 3. To achieve this, we need to transcend the worst things that happen to us. But to make change of this magnitude we need to commit. It is a lifelong commitment and something you will need to work through for the rest of your life. You cannot follow anyone or take the path of those that have walked before because your path will be different. Your reasons for taking the journey are different and your purpose moving forward is different.

There is a story about King Henry and his knights of the round table. They were sent to retrieve a precious item from the centre of the deepest, darkest forest. A forest that was filled with dragons and almost impenetrable. To save time and have the best chance of one of them finding the treasure that was sought, each knight entered the forest at a different point and in an area that had not been penetrated by anyone else. They knew that by following another man's path, they were destined to fail. That they would become entangled by that other man's dragons. They knew that the best way to find the treasure was to take a new path where those dragons could not see them coming.

You are now one of those knights. Your path is untravelled. You will now need to vastly modify your life. Possibly get rid of things that have been in your life for a long-time that you now realise have not been good for you. You will need to work through the method of this book; a method of proven success that in my 20-plus years of rehabilitation consulting and coaching business owners who have experienced injury or ill mental health, has proven to bring the desired outcome: the life transformed.

All the people I have worked with have travelled the journey described in these pages. They have worked through the process to own their circumstance (Chapter 2). They have identified what they want (Chapter 3). Made the necessary changes (Chapter 4). Set goals and focused on the desired result (Chapter 5). And, tapped into their own resources and the resources around them that others can provide and are willing to provide when you demonstrate a willingness to help yourself (Chapter 6).

~ 3 ~

How do I know this? Well, it is not just my experience working to help people rehabilitate after injury or ill mental health, it is because I have lived it. Lived it several times. No, I have never been injured or mentally unwell to a point where I have had to transform my life. I hope I never have to transform under those circumstances, although I believe after helping so many people successfully transform, I have what is needed to do so if those conditions arose. Rather, I have had to transform my life because my situation had become untenable for me and I needed to change my environment or go after something different, to lead the life meant for me. That is why I have stated that this book is not just for people recovering from injury or ill mental health, it is for anyone looking to make a sustainable change. The requirements do not differ.

My first transformation occurred when I was 17. A New Zealander, I grew up in a town called Timaru (a city about the same size as Geelong) and about an hour and half south of Christchurch. I left school after semester one of year 11. School was not for me. I thought I did all right, but as I recalled in Chapter 1, when mum passed away we found all my school reports in a box in the garage, and it appears I was a little deluded. I think I had some Dyslexia. I remember having to go to special one-on-one lessons with a remedial teacher but no one really ever told me what that was about and why. Either way, I never really got school and thus was not very successful.

So, I left school and got a job as an advertising cadet for a newspaper – Herald Communications, which had a circulation of around 360,000. It was a great job selling and designing newspaper adverts in the assistance of the advertising reps. It paid awesomely well at $375 per week, which in 1989 was a fortune for a 17-year-old. I made the most of it. In hindsight I wish I had saved a little more, but hindsight is 20/20. Anyway, I didn't realise I was having too much fun and not doing my job properly. I was called into the CEO's office and told, loud enough for the building to hear that I was a 'useless piece of shit' and that if I did not show some improvement I was out.

Now you must remember that these were the good old days when employees could be yelled at, sworn at and threatened with very little repercussion. It was never a good experience, but most people just brushed it off and took it as valuable feedback. Made the changes necessary and continued with life. Now days an employer would never get away with that and would find themselves at Fair Work Australia settling a stress claim. Those were the days before stress was a recognised factor and so people's mental health after a public spray from the boss was never considered. Either way, whilst it scared me it was the best thing for me at the time.

Remember how earlier in this chapter we discussed the universe sending a message and if you don't listen, the universe will upend you. This was my upending. I went home, considered my behaviour, owned my part in creating the situation, listened to my intuition, made the change in my head, went to work the next day and focused on what had to be done and called upon my colleagues to help. Six months later I was promoted to a features rep and given my own publication to manage the advertising. This was the initiator of my high work ethic today. Thank you Nigel Watt.

My experience at Herald Communications and my transformation was immediate. Sometimes change has to be made quickly in response to an urgent situation. In this case, it was shape up or ship out. My second transformation was longer and came five years later.

During my time with Herald Communications, I would moonlight as a bartender at two or three of the local pubs. After a period, I got asked to manage one of the pubs. So, I left the Herald and did that for about a year. I then threw my hat in the ring for a food and beverage manager role on one of New Zealand's ski fields – Whakapapa. A dormant volcano in the middle of the North Island. That was 1995, the year it came back to life and erupted.

After the eruption, the season got cut short and I went to Wellington to bludge off my sister (15 years older than me) and find a job. It took 48 hours to find a job as a functions and wedding co-ordinator at Wallaceville House, a prestige wedding and function facility. Best year and a half of my life. Great team, fun environment. Despite the fun it was during this time that I realised the hospitality industry was not for me. That intuition thing we have talked about kicked in and I knew I needed to be somewhere else. My calling to injury management and rehabilitation came and I applied to occupational therapy school as a mature-age student (if being 22 years old is mature). And so began my second transformation to become an occupational therapist, to my current career and, ultimately, to write this book for you.

This transformation was longer of course. Four years of education, enduring the twice annual placements. Usually in regional locations that couldn't get OTs, so would offer placements to try and attract some. And because you were expected to get a holistic view of the profession, these placements would often be in areas of absolutely no interest to me: Aged Care, Community Care and hospitals.

Now these are all wonderful areas for OTs who have the calling to these sectors, but for me I always knew I was going into injury management. So, after OT school I did a small stint with a recruitment firm whilst trying to get a job with an insurance company before I finally achieved my four-year-long transformation and joined Aon Risk which, as you read earlier, moved me to Australia and my destiny – doing what I do now.

~ 4 ~

Transforming your life is not isolated to changes in your career. Sometimes it is your personal life that needs to change. Again, you will recall in Chapter 5 we spoke about your environment and the people you surround yourself with. Make sure this environment and the people are conducive to production of positive influence to bring out the best in you.

When I went to OT school, I was followed by my girlfriend at the time (Debbie). Over the four years of training, she hung out with me in Dunedin – a small city about three quarters of the way down the South Island of New Zealand. Ironically, the place I was born. A cold, dismal, hell of a place. In winter, the place is so cold that it is pretty much frost from March until October and every morning they must send the grit trucks out to de-ice the roads. I am surprised that she lasted so long in that place.

During the course of our time in Dunedin, and more from a sense of obligation than pure love (I am a believer that there is a soul mate out there for everyone), I asked her to marry me. No sooner had the words come out of my mouth than I immediately regretted it. Once again, the voice inside me told me it was not the right path.

Debbie left Dunedin after being made redundant from work, and a year before I graduated. Dunedin is not exactly alive with employment, so we decided she was better to go back to Wellington where there were more opportunities. I followed at the end of the year.

On the way home I spent a couple of days at Mum's place (pre-stroke), and told her I was having doubts about my engagement. It was during our conversations about making the right decision and doing the right thing by Debbie that Mum told me, 'There is no right or wrong, there is only decision'. After further discussion I decided to call off the wedding.

For some reason Debbie and I stayed together, but I always had a nagging feeling that it was not right. Some seven years and two houses later I pulled the pin on the relationship and moved to Australia. I pretty much walked away and left her everything. Probably a little silly but finding your place on this Earth is not about money and processions. Don't get me wrong, I like money – it certainly helps. But to find your 'bliss' as Joseph Campbell would say, you're not going to find it with money. Some of the most miserable people in the world are the wealthiest.

That was transformation three. The biggest of the transformations and the toughest up to that point. It is never nice having to break someone else's heart to follow your path. Sometimes it is necessary. My point is, a transformation does not just relate to careers. It can be any part of your life and as big or as small as it needs to be for you to follow your bliss.

'Bliss' is the concept discovered by Joseph Campbell, the prolific American author and editor whose works on comparative mythology examined the universal functions of myth in various human cultures and mythic figures in a wide range of literatures. Hence, the strong references throughout this chapter to Joseph Campbell's work. Campbell philosophised that everybody has a 'bliss', a frame of reference of what their ultimate life would look like. He also believed that everybody should be chasing their bliss and taking every step possible to find it.

I've transformed numerous times since ending my engagement with Debbie, changing my career to get an MBA, becoming a CEO. Realising the view from the top of the corporate ladder was not what it seemed and changed my career again to what I do now. I have had relationships that have not worked. I have had kids and had to transform into a father. Something I am still working on. I got married and had to transform into a husband.

TRANSFORM YOUR LIFE

A work in progress. All I can say is that some things aren't always forever.

On all these transformations, the process has been the same. It has been what you have read in this book. Each time the process has taken me to where I wanted to be at that time or where I wanted to get to. It has worked and that is why I know it works for everyone, injured physically or mentally, or simply when a change is needed. That is why it will work for you.

You see, transformation is constant if you are doing it right. You are always improving, adding new information to your schemas, improving who you are and your situation. It is just that sometimes you are forced into a transformation you didn't plan and, on a magnitude, far bigger than you ever thought you were capable of, like Alan Newey. It is your ability to work through the process in this book that will determine your ability to succeed with that transformation.

~ 5 ~

In the early 2020s I rented a house that had a potted tree on the front porch. An olive tree. The tree had been hidden under the roof of the porch for years. No sun, no water, the soil was dry and void of nutrition. The tree looked like the left side of the tree on the cover of this book. We thought it was dead. But olive trees are hardy plants, hardy just like you. They will lie dormant waiting for the opportunity to transform to their beautiful natural green again.

We watered that plant, turned the soil and moved the pot into the sun. Pretty soon that olive tree transformed and looked more like the right side of the tree on the cover of this book. I know that you have been waiting for an opportunity to be the person you are meant to be, to bloom again like the olive tree and to maximise your time on this planet.

I can't believe I have been on this planet 49 years – it has gone so quickly. I have an estimated 35 years left (assuming nothing catastrophic happens and I can look after my physical and mental health). If it is longer, great! Definitely not shorter – I have too much I still want to do. My point is, we are here such a short time. There is no use living a life of partial happiness. Life should be bliss. If life isn't bliss then it is time to change it. To transform your life.

Throughout this book I have provided you a pathway to transform your life and find your bliss. A pathway that has been tested by many with physical and mental health issues and those that simply don't like the life they live. It is not an easy path. It will require you to take Ownership of your life and the things you have/have not done. It will require you to listen to your Intuition – the life you are supposed to live. You will need to make Change when you are hard-wired for comfort and told by the rest of the world that change is not good. To overcome these negative voices, you will need to Focus. Find your inner-resources and leverage the resources around you. Only you can do that, and when people see you being Self-Reliant, they will help, and things will become easier.

The pathway in this book is tried and tested as you have seen from the stories of David, Mr J, Newey, Peter, Bill Hanagan and Jonathan Yulison. Some of whom have completed the journey, crossed all five bridges, and transformed their lives. Some have stumbled, completed one or more of the bridges, while finding others a bridge too far. They have not been able to make the transformation. I can show you hundreds of other examples too.

From those that have gone the distance we know that this pathway works for anyone and everyone willing to commit to the journey. My mum got captured by her dragons on this pathway. She stumbled at the Bridge of Change. Maybe with my help she would have been able to cross that bridge and live her final years in her bliss. We will never know.

TRANSFORM YOUR LIFE

One thing we do know from all those that have crossed these Five Bridges, is that if you commit and complete the journey, you will Transform Your Life.

REFERENCES

Chapter 1 – My Life

America's Got Talent (2021). What America's Got Talent didn't get a chance to tell you about Jane Marczewski Nightbirde - https://www.youtube.com/watch?v=K9ulEq0-z3M&ab_channel=EpicTopTrending

Australian Institute of Health and Wellness. (2022). Mental Health: Prevalence and Impact. - https://www.aihw.gov.au/reports/australias-health/mental-health

Schwantez, M - Science Says 92 Percent of People Don't Achieve Their Goals. Here's How the Other 8 Percent Do, Inc (July, 2016) - https://www.inc.com/marcel-schwantes/science-says-92-percent-of-people-dont-achieve-goals-heres-how-the-other-8-perce.html

Australian Institute of Health and Welness. (2022). Mental Health Services. - https://www.aihw.gov.au/reports-data/health-welfare-services/mental-health-services/overview

Australian Institute of Health and Welfare (2022). All Causes of Injury. - https://www.aihw.gov.au/reports/australias-health/injury

Summit Performance Psychology. (2022). Peak Recovery Mindset and Mental Health After an Injury - https://summitperformancepsych.com/mental-health-after-injury/

J. G. Black, G. P. Herbison, R. A. Lyons, S. Polinder, S. Derrett; Recovery after injury: an individual patient data meta-analysis of general health status using the EQ-5D. https://pubmed.ncbi.nlm.nih.gov/21986741/

Dictionary (2022). Bridge - https://www.google.com/search?q=what+is+a+bridge

ABS (Australian Bureau of Statistics) 2008. National Survey of Mental Health and Wellbeing: summary of results, 2007. ABS cat. no. 4326.0. Canberra: ABS.

ABS 2018. National Health Survey: first results, 2017–18. ABS cat. no. 4364.0.55.001. Canberra: ABS.

ABS 2019. Forward work program, 2019–20. ABS cat. no. 1006.0. Canberra: ABS.

AHHA (The Australian Healthcare and Hospitals Association) 2019. Investment in health surveys, mental health and prevention money well spent. AHHA. Viewed 9 October 2019.

AIHW (Australian Institute of Health and Welfare) 2016. Australian Burden of Disease Study: impact and causes of illness and death in Aboriginal and Torres Strait Islander people 2011. Cat. no. BOD 7. Canberra: AIHW.

AIHW 2019. Australian Burden of Disease Study: impact and causes of illness and death in Australia 2015. Cat. no. BOD 22. Canberra: AIHW.

AIHW 2020. Mental health services in Australia. Canberra: AIHW.

COAG (Council of Australian Governments) Health Council 2017. The Fifth National Mental Health and Suicide Prevention Plan. Canberra: Department of Health.

Lawrence D, Johnson S, Hafekost J, Boterhoven de Haan K, Sawyer M, Ainley J et al. 2015. The mental health of children and adolescents: report on the second Australian Child and Adolescent Survey of Mental Health and Wellbeing. Canberra: Department of Health.

Morgan VA, Waterreus A, Jablensky A, Mackinnon A, McGrath JJ, Carr V et al. 2011. People living with psychotic illness 2010: report of the second Australian National Survey. Canberra: Department of Health.

Slade T, Johnston A, Teesson M, Whiteford H, Burgess P,

Pirkis J et al. 2009. The mental health of Australians 2: report on the 2007 National Survey of Mental Health and Wellbeing. Canberra: Department of Health and Ageing.

WHO (World Health Organization) 2013. Mental health action plan 2013–2020. Geneva: WHO.

Chapter 2 – Ownership

AZ Quotes (2022). Elisabeth Kubler-Ross Quotes About Choices - https://www.azquotes.com/author/8304-Elisabeth_Kubler_Ross/tag/choices

Wikipedia (2022). Elizabeth Kuber-Ross. - https://en.wikipedia.org/wiki/Elisabeth_K%C3%BCbler-Ross

D. Debuque, & M. Williams (July 2017 – Present) – Ozark. Netflix - https://en.wikipedia.org/wiki/Ozark_(TV_series)#:~:text=Ozark%20is%20an%20American%20crime,the%20Ozarks%20for%20money%20laundering.

N. Shpancer Ph.D. How Therapy Works. What it means to 'process an issue'. Psychology Today (2018). - https://www.psychologytoday.com/us/blog/insight-therapy/201801/how-therapy-works-what-it-means-process-issue

www.themelbournemensgroup.com.au

Chapter 3 – Intuition

Healthline (2021). Everything You Need to Know About Bipolar Disorder - https://www.healthline.com/health/bipolar-disorder

Mayoclinic. (2022). Borderline Personality Disorder - https://www.mayoclinic.org/diseases-conditions/borderline-personality-disorder/symptoms-causes/syc-20370237

J. M. May, MD,1 T. M. Richardi, PsyD,2 and K. S. Barth, DO - Dialectical Behaviour Therapy as Treatment for Borderline Personality Disorder. Ment Health Clin. 2016 Mar; 6(2): 62–67. Published online 2016 Mar 8. doi: 10.9740/mhc.2016.03.62 - https://www.ncbi.nlm.nih.gov/pmc/articles/PMC6007584/

Dr. S McLeod - Maslow's Hierarchy of Needs. Simple Psychology - published 2007, updated December 29, 2020. https://www.simplypsychology.org/maslow.html

T. Robbins - Discover the 6 Human Needs. https://www.tonyrobbins.com/mind-meaning/do-you-need-to-feel-significant/

K. Cherry. (March 2021) - The 5 Levels of Maslow's Hierarchy of Needs. https://www.verywellmind.com/what-is-maslows-hierarchy-of-needs-4136760

G. deBecker (2000). The Gift of Fear. Bloomsbury, Great Britain.

Sunday Night (2012) Ben Roberts-Smith VC MG an Australian Hero part 1 - https://www.youtube.com/watch?v=NWeN-S1CS7yc&ab_channel=AlexGaripoli

Australian War Memorial (2022). Victoria Cross - https://www.awm.gov.au/articles/encyclopedia/vic_cross

Quora (2021). What is the origin of the quote attributed to a Navy SEAL - "Under pressure, you don't rise to the occasion, you sink to the level of your training"? Where and when was this said? - https://www.quora.com/What-is-the-origin-of-the-quote-attributed-to-a-Navy-SEAL-Under-pressure-you-dont-rise-to-the-occasion-you-sink-to-the-level-of-your-training-Where-and-when-was-this-said

Whikipedia (2022). Fight or Flight Response - https://en.wikipedia.org/wiki/Fight-or-flight_response

Chapter 4 – Change

R. Power., 5 Ways to Embrace Change at Work and in Life. Inc, (Jan 2016) - https://www.inc.com/rhett-power/5-ways-to-embrace-change-at-work-and-in-life.html

I. Gura - 12 Reasons Why You Should Seek & Embrace Change. The Daily Positive (March 2019) - https://www.thedailypositive.com/12-reasons-why-you-should-seek-embrace-change/

TEDx Perth - Jason Clarke - Embracing Change. YouTube

(December, 2010) - https://www.youtube.com/watch?v=vPhM-8lxibSU&ab_channel=TEDxTalks

TEDx Mt Hood Salon - Aden Nepom - Embracing Change: Making New Choices Instead of "Safe" Choices. YouTube (August 2019) - https://www.youtube.com/watch?v=3FwWN-77TAMM&ab_channel=TEDxTalks

L. Bettison. - How to Change Your Life by Changing the Stories You Tell Yourself. Tiny Buddha - https://tinybuddha.com/blog/change-life-changing-stories-tell-yourself/

J. Sinrich - 15 Stories That Prove It's Never Too Late to Change Your Life. Readers Digest (July, 2021) - https://www.rd.com/list/never-too-late-change-your-life/

T. Robbins (2021) – Unleash the Power Within: Change Your Story - https://www.tonyrobbins.com/stories/unleash-the-power/change-your-story/

T. Denning. 13 Ways I Totally Changed My Life Story And So Can You. Mission.Org (December 2017) - https://medium.com/the-mission/13-ways-i-totally-changed-my-life-story-and-so-can-you-342e6857def7

N. Tassler - How to Get Better at Dealing with Change. Harvard Business Review (September, 2016) - https://hbr.org/2016/09/how-to-get-better-at-dealing-with-change

Boyer., St Clair & Aull. (April, 2021) – Why can't you remember your car crash - https://www.boyerstpierre.com/blog/2021/04/why-cant-you-remember-your-car-crash/

Cleveland Clinic (2021) – Optic Atrohpy. https://my.clevelandclinic.org/

Cleveland Clinic (2021) – Phantom Limb Pain. https://my.clevelandclinic.org/

www.chatsafety.com.au

Chapter 5 – Focus

S. Bierley (July 2020) – The Greatest: Rafael Nadal – mental and physical giant with a brutal forehand. The Guardian

E. T. Gendlin (August 1982). Focusing. Bantam, New York.

D. A. Sabien. (May 2018) – Focussing for Sceptics.

TEDx Manchester - Chris Bailey - How to Get Your Brain to Focus. YouTube (April 2019) -

T. Robbins - Conor McGregor's Road to Greatness! - Tony Interviews Conor to Find Out What Makes Greatness Possible. YouTube (June 2020)

TEDx Patras - Peter Sage - How To Eliminate Self Doubt Forever & The Power of Your Unconscious Mind. YouTube (January, 2020)

Michalewicz, M. (2013). Life in Half a Second. Hybrid Publishers, Ormond, Australia

Chapter 6 – Self-Reliance

Wikipedia (2021) – Self Reliance.

Emerson, Ralph Waldo (1841). "Familiar Quotations". Bartleby.com (10th ed.). Bartleby Inc. (published 1919).

Baldwin, Neil (2005). The American Revelation. New York, NY: St. Martin's Press. pp. 61-78.

Liang, Haijing (November 2014). "An eye for an – I – An insight into Emerson's thought of self-reliance". Journal of Language Teaching and Research. 4: 1351–1355. CiteSeerX 10.1.1.1020.9270.

Richardson, Robert D., Jr. (1995). Emerson: The mind on fire. Berkeley, California: University of California Press. p. 99. ISBN 0-520-08808-5.

McAleer, John (1984). Ralph Waldo Emerson: Days of encounter. Boston, MA: Little, Brown and Company. p. 105. ISBN 0-316-55341-7.

Sacks, Kenneth S. (2003). Understanding Emerson: "The American scholar" and his struggle for self-reliance. Princeton University Press. ISBN 0-691-09982-0.

Myerson, Joel (2000). Transcendentalism: A reader. New York, NY: Oxford University Press. pp. 318-339.

Hacht, Anne, ed. (2007). The American Dream. "Major Works" Literary Themes for Students. Detroit, MI: Gale. pp. 453–466. Retrieved November 25, 2014.

Zalta, Edward. "Ralph Waldo Emerson". The Stanford Encyclopedia of Philosophy.

Malachuk, Daniel (September 1998). "The Republican Philosophy of Emerson's Early Lectures". New England Quarterly. 71 (3): 404–428. doi:10.2307/366851. Retrieved December 19, 2021.

Emerson, Ralph Waldo (1841). Self-Reliance. Boston, MA: Project Gutenberg (published November 2019).

"individualism". Vocabulary.com (dictionary definition). Retrieved 2019-12-06.

Melville, Herman (1981) [1851]. Arvin, Newton (ed.). Moby-Dick. Bantam. pp. 549-558. ISBN 0-553-21311-3. "[archived source]" – via Internet Archive (archive.org).

Chase, Richard, ed. (1962). "Melville and Moby-Dick". Melville: a Collection of Critical Essays. Spectrum. pp. 56–61.

Cladis, Mark S. (March 2009). "Religion, Democracy, and Virtue: Emerson and the Journey's End". Religion & Literature. 41: 49–82. JSTOR 25676858.

O'Sullivan, Michael (28 August 1998). "Next Stop Wonderland". The Washington Post (film review).

C. Moore – What is Self-Reliance and How to Develop It. Positive Psychology (December 2021) -

K. Eschenroeder – A Man's Guide to Self-Reliance. The Art of Manliness.

Dictionary.com (2021). Self-Reliance. https://www.dictionary.com/browse/self-reliance

A.C. Brooks - The Link Between Self-Reliance and Well-Being. The Atlantic (July 2021) -

www.jessicawatson.com.au/about

Chapter 7 – Transform

Deepak Chopra, Robin Sharma, Rashida Jones, Sir Ken Robinson (March 2020). Finding Joe. - https://www.youtube.com/watch?v=s8nFACrLxr0&ab_channel=PatrickSolomon

www.ingramcontent.com/pod-product-compliance
Lightning Source LLC
Chambersburg PA
CBHW020325010526
44107CB00054B/1983